Die Romantische Straße

vom Main zu den Alpen

The Romantic Road

from the River Main to the Alps

Text: Wolfgang Kootz
Fotos: W. Sauer u.a.

Willi Sauer Verlag

Die Romantische Straße

Bereits an ihrem Ausgangspunkt Würzburg bietet sich dem Besucher mit der Marienburg, dem Käppele, der Mainbrücke, dem Dom und vor allem der fürstbischöflichen Residenz eine grandiose Fülle historischer Kunstschätze. Hier in der mainfränkischen Metropole schufen Riemenschneider, Neumann und Tiepolo unsterbliche Meisterwerke, die auch auf die Orte in ihrer Nachbarschaft ausstrahlten. Nach Süden schließt sich das badische Frankenland mit dem lieblichen Taubertal und seinen sonnigen Rebhängen und idyllischen Winzerorten um Tauberbischofsheim und Lauda-Königshofen an. Seine kunstreichen Gotteshäuser sowie die zahlreichen Heiligenstatuen und Bildstöcke gaben der Landschaft den Beinamen „Madonnenländchen", das auch bekannt ist für seine intakte Natur mit einer artenreichen Flora und Fauna. Der Reiz der Romantischen Straße ist auch in der Vielzahl der kleineren geistlichen und weltlichen Herrscher begründet, die hier residierten. In Bad Mergentheim hinterließen die Hochmeister des Deutschen Ordens ihr Schloss, in Weikersheim waren es die mächtigen Herren von Hohenlohe. Über Röttingen und Creglingen führt die Route durch eines der reizvollsten Täler nach Rothenburg, dem Inbegriff mittelalterlicher Romantik. Hier beginnt eine Reihe ehemaliger freier Reichsstädte, die sich über Feuchtwangen, Dinkelsbühl, Nördlingen bis nach Donauwörth zieht. Ihre Altstadtkerne sind allesamt erfreulich gut erhalten, als habe die Weltgeschichte hier über Jahrhunderte ihren Atem angehalten. Innerhalb dieser Folge sorgen die Kleinresidenzen der Fürsten von Hohenlohe-Schillingsfürst und von Oettingen-Wallerstein ebenso für ständigen Wechsel wie die mächtige Harburg über dem Wörnitztal zwischen der Schwäbischen und der Fränkischen Alb. Südlich der Donau durchreisen wir das Donauried und erreichen das 2000-jährige Augsburg, die einst mächtige Handelsmetropole der Fugger und Welser. Hier lebten und wirkten der Maler Holbein d. Ä. und der Baumeister Elias Holl, schlossen Protestanten und Katholiken 1555 ihren Religionsfrieden, begegnen uns auf Schritt und Tritt Zeugen der großen geschichtlichen Vergangenheit. Etwas abseits liegt Friedberg, die einstige Festungsstadt der bayerischen Wittelsbacher. Während der bisherige Verlauf der Romantischen Straße in etwa der mittelalterlichen Handelsstraße über Würzburg entspricht, verläuft sie ab Augsburg im Wesentlichen auf der Trasse der römischen Militärstraße „Via Claudia", die einst Augsburg mit Rom verband. Sie durchquert das Lechfeld, auf dem im Jahre 955 Otto der Große die Ungarn besiegte und sie dadurch von Mitteleuropa fernhielt. Wir besichtigen Landsberg und Hohenfurch, ehe wir bei Schongau in den "Pfaffenwinkel" einkehren, ein Gebiet wie ein Freilicht-

The Romantic Road

Right from its start-point in Würzburg, which boasts the Marienburg, the Käppele, the old bridge over the River Main, the cathedral, and first and foremost the residential palace of the Prince-Bishops, the Romantic Road offers the visitor a cornucopia of historic artistic treasures. This is the capital of the Franconian Main region, and here artists like Riemenschneider, Neumann, and Tiepolo created immortal masterpieces which often radiate their beauty into other towns and villages in the district. The region to the south is the Baden part of Franconia, with the charming valley of the River Tauber and its sunny vineyards around Tauberbischofsheim and Lauda-Königshofen. The richness of the works of arts in its churches and the innumerable statues of saints and of the Saviour have given this district the name of Madonnenländchen, the „Little Madonna-land"; it is also famous for its unspoilt natural beauty and the diversity of its flora and fauna. The charm of the Romantic Road also stems from the large number of minor rulers, both spiritual and worldly, that used to reside here. The High Masters of the Deutscher Orden, an Order of chivalry, left their castle to posterity in Bad Mergentheim , as did the powerful Lords of Hohenlohe in Weikersheim. The route leads through Röttingen and Creglingen and one of the most charming of river valleys to Rothenburg ob der Tauber, the quintessence of romantic medieval towns. This is the start of a long line of former Free Imperial Cities running through Feuchtwangen, Dinkelsbühl, and Nördlingen to Donauwörth. Their historic town centres are, without exception, so well preserved that you might think that history had held its breath here. In between these towns there are the minor residences of the Princes of Hohenlohe-Schillingsfürst and of Oettingen-Wallerstein providing variety just as much as does the massive Harburg castle, high above the Wörnitz valley between the Swabian and the Franconian Alb. South of the Danube we travel through the Donauried and reach Augsburg, a city 2,000 years old and once the centre of the trading empires of the Fugger and the Welser merchant dynasties. This is where the painter Holbein the Elder worked, and the architect Elias Holl, where Protestants and Catholics signed their peace treaty in 1555, and where every step we take brings us face to face with testimony of the city's grand historical past. A little way to one side of our route is Friedberg, once the fortified city of the Bavarian Wittelsbach royal dynasty. Whereas the Romantic Road up to now has run more or less along the medieval trading road through Würzburg, from Augsburg onwards it runs mainly along the line of the Roman military road, the via claudia, which once linked Augsburg with Rome. It runs across the Lechfeld, the battlefield where Otto the Great

museum der sakralen Kunst in Klöstern und Kirchen, ausgestattet mit unnachahmlichen Malereien und Stuckarbeiten der großen Wessobrunner Meister. Höhepunkt ist der Welt schönste Rokokokirche, die Wies. Lediglich die beiden berühmtesten Königsschlösser Bayerns bei Schwangau machen ihr im Publikumsinteresse Konkurrenz: das romanisch ausgebaute Hohenschwangau und – gegenüber – das Märchenschloss König Ludwigs II., Neuschwanstein. Auch die Natur stimmt in den grandiosen Schlussakkord der Romantischen Straße mit ein und steuert Wiesen und Wälder, Seen und Bergketten als Kulisse für die herrlichen Bauwerke bei. Die Route endet schließlich in Füssen im Ostallgäu, nur einen Steinwurf von der Grenze nach Österreich entfernt. Wer diese herrliche Touristenstraße offenen Auges durchfahren und diesen fast unerschöpflichen Reichtum kulturellen Erbes erlebt hat, wird dankbar sein, dass uns unsere Ahnen ein solches Übermaß an Kunstwerken hinterlassen haben. Ebenso ist unsere Generation aufgerufen, alles zu tun, diese Fülle von Überliefertem unversehrt an unsere Nachkommen weiterzureichen.

defeated the Hungarians in 955 and thus drove them out of Central Europe. We visit Landsberg and Hohenfurch before reaching Schongau and entering the Pfaffenwinkel, a region that is almost an open-air museum in its own right with monasteries and churches containing the inimitable paintings and stucco work of the great Wessobrunn masters. The highpoint is the most beautiful rococo church in the world, the Wieskirche. In terms of public interest, its only rivals are the royal Bavarian castles near Schwangau: the romantically extended Hohenschwangau and, opposite it, King Ludwig II's fairy-tale castle of Neuschwanstein. Even Nature played some of the notes in the closing chord of the Romantic Road, contributing meadows and forests, and lakes and chains of mountains, as the back-drop to these magnificent buildings. The route finally ends in Füssen, in the eastern Allgäu, only a stone's throw from the Austrian border. Anyone who has travelled along this magnificent tourist route with eyes open to see the almost inexhaustible wealth of our cultural inheritance will be thankful that our forefathers have bequeathed such a plethora of works of art to us.

Deutschland: Im südlichen Teil, besonders markiert, die 350 km lange Romantische Straße zwischen Würzburg und Füssen

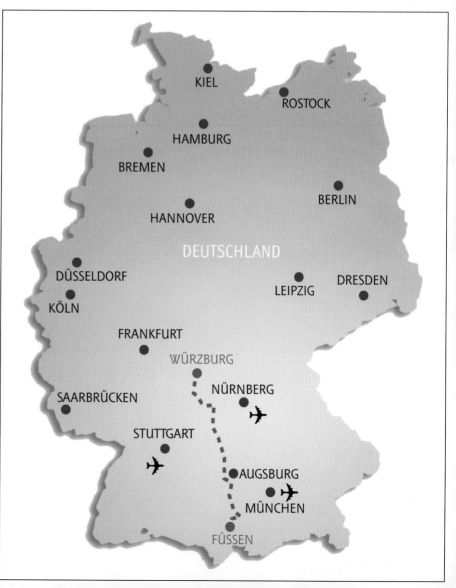

Germany, showing the main routes. The Romantic Road has been added with special emphasis

Würzburg

Die ehemalige Residenz der Fürstbischöfe besitzt trotz der Zerstörungen durch einen Bombenangriff 1945 eine Vielzahl von Kulturschätzen internationaler Bedeutung, das Residenzschloss wurde 1982 in die „UNESCO-Liste des Erbes der Welt" aufgenommen.

Die erste christliche Kirche der Stadt, gleichzeitig nach dem Dom von Trier die älteste Deutschlands, wurde 706 zu Ehren der Muttergottes geweiht. Nach ihr nennt man den „Würzberg" auch heute noch **Marienberg**, ebenso wie die Burg, die ab 1201 dort entstand. Bis zum Bau der Stadtresidenz (18. Jh.) diente sie den Fürstbischöfen als Wohnsitz und Schutzschild gegen die immer wieder nach Reichsfreiheit strebenden Bürger. Erst 1631 gelang Gustav Adolf von Schweden die erste Eroberung. Ab 1642 wurde sie zur Reichsfestung ausgebaut, die Mehrzahl der heutigen Baulichkeiten erhielt ihre heutige Gestalt. Darin ist heute das Mainfränkische Museum untergebracht, das neben einer Sammlung sakraler Kunst und Zeugnissen fränkischer Weinkultur einen Überblick über das Werk des Holzschnitzers Tilman Riemenschneider zeigt. Der berühmte und angesehene

Die Festung Marienberg mit dem „Alten Kranen"

Würzburg

The former seat of the Prince-Bishops possesses a cornucopia of cultural treasures of international importance, despite all the destruction of the 1945 air raid, and in 1982 the Residential Palace was added to the UNESCO World Heritage List.

The first Christian church in the city, sharing with Trier cathedral the position of Germany's oldest church, was consecrated to the Glory of the Mother of God in 706, for which reason the hill on which it stands, the „Würzberg", is still called the **Marienberg**, as is the castle that was built on it from 1201 onwards. Until the Stadtresidenz or Residential Palace was built in the 18th century, the castle served as the prince-bishops' residence and protective shield against the citizens and their recurrent demands for legal freedom. It was not until 1631 that it was first conquered, by Gustav Adolf of Sweden. It was extended into an Imperial Fortress in 1642, when most of the buildings took on their present-day shape. Nowadays they house parts of the State Archive, a small congress centre, a restaurant, the Fürstenbau museum, and the Main / Franconian Museum, which in addition

The castle of Marienberg was the residence of the Prince-Bishops of Würzburg

Festung Marienberg mit Kiliansturm und Scheren-bergtor

Marienberg fortress with Kiliansturm and Scheren-bergtor

Festung Marienberg: zierliches Brunnenhaus der Renaissance von 1603

Marienberg fortress: Fountain house of the renaissance built 1603

Künstler lebte 48 Jahre in Würzburg, war hier Ratsherr und später Bürgermeister. Während des Bauernkrieges 1525 sympathisierte er mit den Bauern und wurde nach deren Niederlage gefoltert und gefangen gehalten. Kurze Zeit nach seiner Freilassung starb er 1531 als gebrochener Mann.

Vom **Fürstengarten** hat der Besucher einen herrlichen Blick auf die Altstadt jenseits des Mains mit der Alten Mainbrücke, den hoch aufragenden Türmen des alten Rathauses, des Doms und der anderen Kirchen sowie dem mächtigen Komplex des Residenzschlosses. Vom südlich gelegenen Nikolausberg grüßt die **Wallfahrts-kapelle „Käppele"**, die noch heute von frommen Pilgern besucht wird. Die **Alte Mainbrücke** erhielt ihre heutige Form im 18. und 19. Jahrhundert, doch enthält sie Bauteile aus der Zeit Bischof Burkhards (8.Jh.). Sie gefällt durch die 12 überlebensgroßen Barockfiguren von Heiligen und Herrschern. Der Turm des Grafeneckart war einst Wohnsitz eines wohlhabenden bischöflichen Beamten. Die beiden unteren Geschosse des Gebäudes

to a collection of works of church art and objects bearing witness to the Franconian art of wine-growing also gives a complete view of the works of the wood-carver Tilman Riemenschneider. This famous and respected artist lived in Würzburg for 48 years and was a councillor, and later Mayor. During the Peasants' Revolt of 1525 he sided with the rebels, and after the revolt had been put down he was tortured and imprisoned. He died in 1531, a broken man, shortly after his release.

The **Old Main** bridge took on its present-day form in the 18th and 19th centuries, although it contains masonry dating from the time of Bishop Burkhard (8th century). Its most pleasing feature is the 12 giant baroque figures of saints and rulers. To our left soars the tower of the Grafeneckart, once the residence of a wealthy official at the Prince-Bishop's court. The two lower storeys of the building have been used as a **town hall** since 1316, the upper ones being added in the 15th and 16th centuries. Immediately adjoining the chapel, the eye is caught by the rich stucco façade of the Falkenhaus, built in

Blick über den Main auf Würzburgs Altstadt

View across the Main to the old city centre of Würzburg

dienen seit 1316 als **Rathaus**, das man im 15. und 16. Jahrhundert aufstockte.

Gleich neben der gotischen Marienkapelle fällt die reiche Stuckfassade des **Falkenhauses** ins Auge, 1751 als Wohnhaus eines wohlhabenden Bürgers geschaffen. Es beherbergt heute das städtische Kulturamt, eine Tourist-Information sowie die Stadtbücherei.

Ganz nahe steht der originelle **„Häckerbrunnen"** mit der Darstellung eines alten Winzers mit Hacke und Weinkrug. Im stimmungsvollen Lusamgärtchen befindet sich unter den Resten des romanischen Kreuzgangs das Epitaph des berühmtesten deutschsprachigen Minnesängers, Walthers von der Vogelweide (gest. 1230), der hier aus dem Besitz des Neumünsterstifts ein Alterslehen erhalten hatte. Im Gotteshaus selbst ruhen die Gebeine des hl. Kilian in einem Steinsarg.

Nachdem die Marienkirche auf dem Berg ab 742 Bistumskirche geworden war, wurde 788 in Anwesenheit

1751 as the home of a wealthy citizen. Nowadays it accommodates the Municipal Culture Office, a Tourist Information Office, and the city library.

Just next to it stands the original **Häckerbrunnen**, representing an old winegrower with a pick and a winejug. Under the remains of the Roman-style crossing is the epitaph of Walther von der Vogelweide, the most famous of all German Minnesängers or medieval bards. He had been granted an fiefdom in his old age from the possessions of the Neumünster monastery. The church itself is the last resting-place of the mortal remains of St Kilian, in a stone coffin.

After the church of St Mary, up on the hill, had become the seat of a Bishop in 742, the first **cathedral** within the city was built in 788 in the presence of Charlemagne himself. The oldest Roman-style parts of the present Cathedral of St Kilian was built at the end of the Domstrasse in about 1050. Further extensions and

Karls des Großen der erste **Dom** innerhalb der Stadt erbaut. Um 1050 entstanden die ältesten, romanischen Teile des heutigen Kiliansdoms am Ende der Domstraße. In den folgenden Jahrhunderten folgten Um- und Ausbauten in Gotik und Spätgotik, Barock und Spätbarock. Bischöfliche Grabdenkmäler des 12. bis 20. Jahrhunderts zieren das Gotteshaus. Der Dreiflügelbau der „**Residenz**", wurde 1982 von der UNESCO als „Weltkulturgut" eingestuft. Der Frankoniabrunnen verliert sich fast in der Weite des Residenzplatzes, Symbol für den Abstand zwischen Fürst und Bürger. Am Fuß der Brunnensäule sitzen die drei berühmtesten Würzburger:

additional building followed over the course of the centuries, in the Gothic, Late Gothic, baroque, and late baroque styles. Tombs of the bishops dating from the 12th to the 20th century decorate the church. The artistically most valuable ones are those of Prince-Bishop Rudolf von Scherenberg (died 1495) and Lorenz von Bibra (died 1519), these two being the work of Tilman Riemenschneider, and also the older gravestones of Otto von Wolfskeel (died 1345). Some of the statues are also the work of Riemenschneider's hand. The mausoleum of the bishops is still the sepulchre at the end of the south nave. The Franconia Fountain is almost lost in the wide

Silhouette der Altstadt von der Mainbrücke

Silhouette of the old town from the Main bridge

Barocke Stuckfassade am Falkenhaus, dahinter die Marienkapelle

Baroque stucco facade on the Falkenhaus, behind it St. Mary's Chapel

Die Südseite des ehemaligen Hofgartens des barocken Residenzschlosses der Fürstbischöfe

The former Court garden of the baroque Residential Palace of the Prince-Bishops

der Minnesänger Walther von der Vogelweide, der Maler Matthias Gothardt Neithardt, bekannt als Matthias Grünewald, und der Bildhauer Tilman Riemenschneider. Die Schlossführung beginnt am Haupteingang des Mittelbaus, der die bedeutendsten der insgesamt 345 Räume der Anlage birgt, nicht gerechnet die riesigen Weinkeller darunter. Verantwortlicher Architekt des 1720 begonnenen Bauwerks war Balthasar Neumann, dem neben einer ausgewogenen Architektur eine Meisterleistung der Statik gelang. Als Sensation galt damals das freitragende Muldengewölbe von 18x32 m, welches das **Treppenhaus** überspannt. Besonders in der Bombennacht von 1945 bewies es seine Standfestigkeit, als es als eines der wenigen Gebäudeteile erhalten blieb. Neben Neumann gelang auch dem italienischen Maler Tiepolo hier der Höhepunkt seines Schaffens, als er das Gewölbe mit dem größten Fresko der Welt schmückte und gleichzeitig ein Kunstwerk höchster Güte schuf. Er stellte die damals bekannten 4 Erdteile symbolisch dar, die den Fürstbischöfen in Würzburg – im Mittelpunkt der Welt – huldigen. Ebenso wie hier überstanden Neumanns Gewölbe und Tiepolos Fresko im **Kaisersaal** die Bombennacht unbeschädigt. Hier stellte der Maler die Hochzeit Friedrich Barbarossas mit Beatrix von Burgund

open spaces of the Residenzplatz, which symbolises the distance between the prince and the citizens. At the foot of the column in the middle of the fountain sit Würzburg's three most famous citizens: the minstrel Walther von der Vogelweide, the painter Matthias Gothardt Neithardt alias Matthias Grünewald, and the sculptor Tilman Riemenschneider. A conducted tour of the palace starts at the main entrance in the central building, which houses the most famous of the total of 345 rooms (not counting the gigantic wine-cellar underneath it). The architect responsible for the work, which began in 1720, was Balthasar Neumann, who succeeded in producing not only perfectly balanced architecture but also a masterpiece of structural calculation. The curved vault spanning the staircase and measuring 18 metres by 32 without any intermediate support was regarded at the time as a sensation. Its sturdy construction was put to the test during the 1945 air raid, when it was one of the few buildings to remain standing. Not only Neumann but also the Italian painter Tiepolo achieved the climax of his creativity here, decorating the vaulted ceiling with a fresco which is the largest in the world and at the same time artistic work of the highest value. He made a symbolic representation

(Würzburg 1156) und die Beleihung des Bischofs mit der Herzogswürde (Reichstag zu Würzburg 1168) dar. Überreich geschmückt ist auch die **Hofkirche** im Südflügel, deren Gemälde der Seitenaltäre Tiepolo schuf. Sie ist heute die beliebteste Hochzeitskirche Würzburgs, und es ist keine Seltenheit, dass sich hier an Wochenenden mehr als 20 Brautpaare das Ja-Wort geben.

of the four parts of the known world paying homage to the Prince-Bishops of Würzburg as the central point of the world. Here again, Neumann's vault and Tiepolo's frescoes survived the air raid unscathed. The painter here illustrated the marriage of Friedrich Barbarossa and Beatrice of Burgundy (Würzburg, 1156).

Residenz: das prunkvolle Treppenhaus mit den Stuckarbeiten und dem berühmten Deckengemälde

The Residential Palace: the imposing staircase with the magnificent stucco work and the famous ceiling paintings

Der Kaisersaal: die Hochzeit Kaiser Friedrich Barbarossas mit Beatrix von Burgund

The Enferos room: the wedding of emperor Friedrich Barbarossa with Beatrix of Burgund

Der Grüne Salon, eines der Paradezimmer

Residenz: Spiegelsaal

The Green Salon, one of the prestigious rooms

The Residential Palace: Hall of Mirrors

Der Würzburger Dom im Herbstnebel

The Würzburger Cathedral in autumn fog

Nahe **Wertheim** und der A3 liegt das Einkaufsdorf **Wertheim Village**. Die Flaniermeile beherbergt mehr als 50 Geschäfte mit einer Vielzahl von Mode- und Designermarken, die mit attraktiven Service-Angeboten (Kinderwagen, Rollstühle, kostenloser Pendelbus in die Altstadt von Wertheim) um Kunden werben. Zur Fußgängerzone gehören auch ein italienisches Restaurant und ein amerikanischer Coffeeshop.

Near **Wertheim,** in the **Wertheim Village** are more than 50 shops with a wide variety of brand articles attract customers thanks to their moderate prices and a big offer of services such as prams, wheel-chairs, free shuttle service to Wertheim historical centre. In the pedestrian precinct you can find an Italian restaurant and an American coffee shop, too.

Tauberbischofsheim

Funde beweisen, dass im Taubergrund bei Tauberbischofsheim bereits um 5500 v. Chr. Siedlungen bestanden. Schon um 730 begann die Christianisierung durch Bonifatius, der um 735 das erste Frauenkloster Deutschlands gründete.

Seine Verwandte, Lioba, war Äbtissin. Beide werden als Stadtheilige verehrt. Von 1237-1803 gehörte die Stadt zum Mainzer Erzbistum, ehe sie 1806 zu Baden gelangte. Noch 1939 hatte sie ganze 3609 Einwohner, doch durch die Ansiedlung von Industrie und 6 Eingemeindungen wuchs sie bis heute auf ca. 14.300 Einwohner an. Als Verwaltungssitz und Wirtschaftszentrum des Main-Tauber-Kreises beherbergt sie die entsprechenden Behörden, ohne ihr Image als „gastliche Stadt im Grünen" opfern zu müssen.

Berühmt wurde Tauberbischofsheim durch den erfolgreichsten Fechtclub der Welt mit Emil Beck als Trainer und „Medaillenschmied". Aus seiner Schule erwuchsen das Bundes- und Landesleistungszentrum – mit Teilinternat –, gleichzeitig als Olympiastützpunkt anerkannt. Viele Freunde hat auch der Frankenwein, der hierzulande in die "Bocksbeutel" abgefüllt wird.

Blick über Tauberbischofsheim, eingebettet in sanfte Berglandschaft

Tauberbischofsheim

The conversion to Chritianity and the first nunnery began in 735 in this town. The names of two of the churches act as a reminder of the two saints. From 1237 to 1803 the town belonged to the See of Mainz, before being transferred to Baden in 1806. In 1939 it still only had 3,609 inhabitants, but the arrival of industry and the integration of six surrounding parishes has now brought that figure up to about 14.300. It is the county town of Main-Tauber County and thus home to the usual administrative authorities, but this does not deprive it of its image as a „hospital little country town."

Tauberbischofsheim rose to fame through the most famous fencing club in the world, with Emil Beck as its trainer and „medalmaking machine". His school of fencing is now recognised as the State and Federal Competitive Centre, which even includes its own boarding school, and as the training base for Olympic competitors. In addition to many other leisure facilities in the town, the fencing club also offers amateurs an opportunity of training during the holidays.

A walk through the old town centre gives the visitor an enduring impression of a historical past, the witnesses

View to Tauberbischofsheim surrounded by soft hill landscape

Der romantische Marktplatz von Tauberbischofs-heim mit Rathaus

The romantics, rural market place of Tauberbischofs-heim, with the town hall

Ein Gang durch die Altstadt vermittelt dem Besucher einen bleibenden Eindruck von der geschichtlichen Vergangenheit, deren Zeugen Generationen von Bürgern sorgsam bewahrt haben. Um den **Marktplatz** gruppieren sich neben dem neugotischen Rathaus (mit Tourist-Information) der barocke Rehhof (1702) sowie drei prächtige Fachwerkbauten. Genau gegenüber dem Barockhaus und 100 Jahre älter ist die Alte Post, einst Abfertigungsgebäude der Thurn- und Taxis'schen Post. Die Sternapotheke am südlichen Ende der Zeile ist mit dem Haus des Wundarztes Franck zusammengebaut.

of which have been lovingly preserved by its inhabitants. The group of buildings around the **market place** include not only the neo-Gothic town hall (which houses the Tourist Information Office) but also the baroque Rehhof (1702) and three magnificent half-timbered houses. Exactly opposite this baroque building, but 100 years older, is the Alte Post, once the despatch office of the postal monopoly run by the Princes of Turn & Taxis. The old chemist's shop, the Sternapotheke, is in the same house as the that of Dr Franck, an early surgeon. Here was the birthplace of the grandfather

Das Kurmainzische Schloss (12. Jh.) mit dem mächtigen Türmersturm beherbergt heute das Tauberfränkische Landschaftsmuseum

The Kurmainzische Castle (from 1250 onwards) with its massive Türmer's Tower is nowadays the home of the Tauber-Franconian Rural Museum

Hier wurde der spätere Conferenzrat Franck, genannt de la Roche, geboren, der Großvater der Romantiker Clemens von Brentano und Bettina von Arnim. Interessante Bürgerhäuser sind das Haus Rincker (1628, mit „Neidkopf" am Giebel) sowie in der östlichen Hauptstraße das Haus Makkert (1744, Barockpalais eines Weinhändlers) und das Lieblerhaus (1628, Holztafeln mit Melusinendarstellungen). Die **Liobakirche** an der Südostecke des Marktplatzes gehörte bis zu seiner Auflösung 1829 dem Franziskanerkloster. Sie wurde 1735 im Stil des Barock umgebaut.

Etwas abseits stehen die Sebastianuskapelle, ein 1476 erstellter doppelstöckiger Bau, sowie die neugotische Stadtkirche St. Martin, die in ihrem Innern wertvolle mittelalterliche Kunstwerke enthält.

Das **Kurmainzische Schloss** ist zwischen dem 11. und 16. Jahrhundert in drei Bauabschnitten entstanden und diente den Amtmännern von Mainz als Sitz. An sie erinnern zahlreiche Wappen mit dem Rad. Im Innern des Schlosses befindet sich seit 1970 das „Tauberfränkische

of the romantic poet Clemens von Brentano; he later held the high rank of Conferenzrat and the aristocratic name of de la Roche. Other interesting patrician houses are Haus Rincker (1628, with the Neidkopf or Jealous Head in the gable) and, at the eastern part of the Hauptstrasse the Haus Mackert (1744, the baroque palace of wine merchant), and the Lieblerhaus (1628, with its wainscoting and depictions of Melusines). The **church of St Lioba**, in the south-eastern corner of the market square, belonged to the Franciscan monastery until the latter was dissolved in 1829. It was rebuilt in the baroque style in 1735.

A little to one side, and to the north, is St Sebastian's chapel, a two-storey building put up in 1746, and the neo-Gothic church of St Martin, the interior of which contains valuable works of medieval art.

The **Kurmainzisches Schloss** or manor house was built in 1595. Parts of this manor-house had been built in 1250, but the main building dates from 1400 and was the seat of the ruling officials appointed from Mainz.

Landschaftsmuseum". Südlich des Schlossplatzes, der vom imposanten **Türmersturm**, dem Wahrzeichen der Stadt, beherrscht wird, finden wir letzte Reste der mittelalterlichen Stadtmauer sowie einen Brunnen mit der „Bischemer Kröte", einer Darstellung des Spitznamens der Einwohner.

Immer wieder trifft man auf gepflegte Grünanlagen und zahlreiche Brunnen, weiter in den Außenbezirken auf ungezählte Bildstöcke und Heiligenstatuen hier im Zentrum des so genannten „Madonnenländchens".

Numerous coats-of-arms which include Mainz's symbol, the wheel, commemorate them. The interior of the building has housed the Tauber-Franconian Rural Museum since 1970. South of the Schlossplatz, which is dominated by the imposing **„Türmer's Tower"**, we find the last remains of the medieval town wall and a fountain illustrating the Bischemer Kröte.

All over the town you will find lovingly manicured parks and gardens and numerous fountains, and on the outskirts there are innumerable wayside shrines and statues of saints; this is the centre of the so-called „Madonna Country".

Fußgängerzone

Pedestrian walk

Tauberfränkisches Landschaftsmuseum

Tauber-Franconian Rural Museum

Spezialität: „der Turmwächter"

The „tower guard"

Lauda-Königshofen

In Gerlachsheim, einem Stadtteil von Lauda-Königshofen, sollten wir die ehemalige Prämonstratenserkirche
(1723-1770) besichtigen, einen herrlichen Barockbau
mit eindrucksvollen Stuckaturen, Altären und Bild-
folgen, ihrer üppig verzierten Kanzel im Rokokostil
sowie der prachtvollen Orgel (1754). Ein romantisches
Fleckchen ist die steinerne Grünbachbrücke mit ihren
überlebensgroßen Heiligenfiguren. Zusammen mit dem
Kloster und den zahlreichen Bildstöcken dokumentie-
ren sie eindrucksvoll den Namen dieses Landstrichs,
„Madonnenländchen".

Hauptort der Kommune ist **Lauda**, als älteste Hochburg
der fränkisch-alemannischen Fasnacht (seit 1545) weithin berühmt. Er besitzt jedoch auch einen sehenswerten
Stadtkern, dessen Häuser aus dem 17. und 18. Jahrhundert vielfach eine Madonnenstatue schmückt. Aus dem
16. Jahrhundert stammen das **Rathaus** und das **Weinbauernhaus**, heute Heimatmuseum mit Sammlungen

Gerlachsheim mit der Grünbachbrücke

Lauda-Königshofen

In Gerlachsheim, which is administratively part of Lauda-Königshofen. Here we ought to look at the church
(1723-1770), which once belonged to the former Prä-
monstraten Order, a missionary Order that took its name
from the French abbey of Prémontré. It is a magnificent
baroque building with impressive stucco work, altars,
and sequences of pictures, luxuriantly decorated rococo-
style pulpit, and a superb organ (1754). The stone bridge
over the Grünbach forms a romantic nook, with its gigantic statues of saints. If one considers this together
with the numerous monasteries and wayside shrines,
one can see impressive documentary proof of the name
of this stretch of countryside, the „Madonna Country".
The main centre of this rural community is **Lauda**, the
oldest „citadel" of the Franconian / Allemannic Fasnacht
– the semi-pagan, semi-Christian spring ceremonies
before the start of Lent. However, it also possesses a
town centre worth seeing, with many 17th and 18th cen-

Gerlachsheim with the Grünbach bridge

Blick durch die Pfarrgasse auf den Kirchturm

View of the church tower across Pfarrgasse

Lauda-Königshofen: Oberes Tor

Lauda-Königshofen: upper gate

aus Weinbaukultur, bäuerlichem Leben, Handwerk, Eisenbahngeschichte und Fasnachtstradition. Reste der Stadtbefestigung wie das Obere Tor und der Pulverturm sowie das Dampflokdenkmal zeugen von der Bedeutung der Stadt. Hübsche ehemalige Winzerdörfer sind auch die Stadtteile Oberlauda und Marbach, vor allem aber **Beckstein**, südlich von Lauda. Mehrfach mit Medaillen ausgezeichnet, präsentiert sich der schmucke Ort gastfreundlich inmitten der Rebhänge, welche die wirtschaftliche Basis für die Bevölkerung liefern. Im Stadtteil **Königshofen** zeugen einige sehenswerte Fachwerkhäuser wie der turmähnliche „Goten" und das „Hohe Haus" vom Bürgerstolz früherer Generationen.

tury houses decorated with depictions of the Madonna. The **town hall** and the **Weinbauernhaus**, or vintners' house, date from the 16th century; today they house the museum of local arts and crafts with its collections of wine-growing and wine-making implements and relics of rustic life, handicrafts, railway history, and the Fasnacht tradition. There are more unspoilt wine-making villages: Oberlauda, Marbach, and of course **Beckstein**, south of Lauda. Distinguished with many medals, this pretty village makes a welcoming sight nestling in the midst of the terraced vineyards which provide the local population with their livelihood.

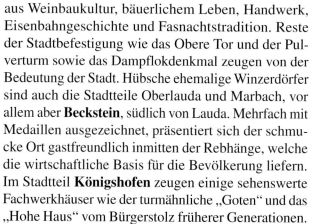

Bad Mergentheim

Der Ort entwickelte sich aus einer fränkischen Siedlung und wurde 1340 zur Stadt erhoben. Im ehemaligen **Residenzschloss** der Hoch- und Deutschmeister (1527-1809) ist heute das **Deutschordensmuseum** untergebracht. Ein Rundgang zur Geschichte des Deutschen Ordens schließt einen Gang über die Empore der Schlosskirche (1730-36 Neubau durch Franz Joseph Roth) und durch die prächtige Fürstenwohnung ein. Um den **Marktplatz** scharen sich schmucke Fachwerkhäuser und Barockpalais sowie das Rathaus (1564). Davor steht der achteckige Renaissance-Brunnen mit einer Statue des Deutschmeisters Wolfgang Schutzbar, genannt „Milchling". Der Hochmeister, der Mergentheim zur Residenz des Deutschen Ordens erhob, war Walter von Cronberg (1527-1543), der Vorgänger des Wolfgang Schutzbar. In der mehrfach umgebauten **Marienkirche** sind noch Wandmalereien aus der Zeit des Kirchenbaus (ab 1300) erhalten. Auch viele Häuser der

Ehemaliges Residenzschloss der Hoch- und Deutschmeister (1527-1809)

Bad Mergentheim

The town originally developed from the Court of a Franconian king at the crossing-point of major trade routes. The town remained in the Order's possession until the conclusion of the Imperial Deputation in 1809, having been maintained as a **residence** since 1527. Their palace nowadays houses a **museum** reflecting the history of the Order and the town. The Meistergemächer, the suite occupied by the Masters of the Order, and the fine Chapter Room are samples of the princely way of life during the baroque, rococo, and classical periods. The **market square** is almost hemmed in by fine half-timbered buildings and baroque palaces, as well as the town hall (1564). In front of it is the octagonal Renaissance fountain with a Statue of the Deutschmeister, Wolfgang Schutzbar, also known as the „Milchling". It was he who elevated Mergentheim to the status of a Residenz in 1526. **St Mary's church**, still contains wall-paintings from the time of its first construction

Former Residencial palace of the Hoch- und Deutschmeister 1527-1809

Residenzschloss, im Hintergrund die Schlosskirche   *Residence with the castle church*

Blick über den Marktplatz

View over the market square

Zimmer im Schloss

Room in the castle

stimmungsvollen Altstadtgassen mit ihren Madonnen-statuen, Heiligenfiguren und farbigen Wappen weisen auf die Herrschaft des Ordens hier im „Herrgottsländle" hin. Bad Mergentheim hat sich seit dem vorigen Jahrhundert zum Kurbad entwickelt. Dies wurde durch einen Schäfer ermöglicht, der 1826 eine längst verschüttete und in Vergessenheit geratene Bittersalzquelle wiederentdeckte, die heute die Anziehungskraft des Heilbades für Stoffwechselstörungen ausmacht. Anziehungspunkt für Kurgäste und Erholungssuchende ist auch der **Kurpark**, dessen Wandelhalle sich besonders bei feuchtem Wetter großer Beliebtheit erfreut. Im Sommer fasziniert der gepflegte und ausgedehnte Rosengarten die Parkbesucher.

(from 1300 onwards). Many other buildings along the enchanting Altstadtgassen, with their Madonna figures, statues of saints, and colourful coats-of-arms, indicate the dominance of the Order here in Herrgottsländle, God's Little Country. (Almost any town with Badinits nameis a spa, where people „take the waters" and enjoy a long ,healthy holiday with medical treatment called a Kur.) This was made possible by a Shepherd who, in 1826 rediscovered a bitter-salt springthat had long been burien and forgotten. In summer, visitors are always fascinated by the carefully maintained and extensive rose garden. The **Wildpark** or Wildlife park, one of Europe's leading parks in terms of the number of local

Impressionen im Kurpark
Impressions in the park

Der nahe **Wildpark** ist der artenreichste Heimattier-Park Europas. Angeschlossen ist ein Heimattier-Museum mit einer umfangreichen Sammlung von Insekten, Schmetterlingen und Vogeleiern.

Eines der berühmtesten Bilder des Mittelalters befindet sich in der Seitenkapelle der Pfarrkirche des Ortsteils **Stuppach**. Die „Stuppacher Madonna" entstand 1519 unter den Händen des Künstlers Mathis Nithardt, heute bekannt unter dem Namen Matthias Grünewald, dem neben Dürer bedeutendsten deutschen Maler. Das spätgotische Marienbild, gefertigt in Kaseinfarben, war fast 300 Jahre im Besitz der Deutschmeister in Bad Mergentheim gewesen, ehe es Pfarrer Blumhofer 1812 aus dem Nachlass des 1806 aufgelösten Ordens für die Kirche in Stuppach erwarb.

species it houses. It includes a museum of local fauna with an extensive collection of insects, butterflies, and birds' eggs.

One of the most famous pictures of the Middle Ages can be found in the side-chapel of the parish church in the adjacent village of **Stuppach**. The Stuppach Madonna was created in 1519 by the hands of the artist Mathis Nithardt, known today by the name of Matthias Grünewald, the greatest German painter and sculptor after Dürer. This late Gothic representation of the Virgin Mary was painted in casein colours and remained almost 300 years in the possession of the Deutschmeister in Bad Mergentheim until Pastor Blumhofer acquired it for the Stuppach church in 1812 from the assets of the Order after its dissolution in 1806.

Die Stuppacher Madonna (Matthias Grünewald) 1519

Stuppach parish church: Madonna (Matthias Gründewald) 1519

<- **Wildtierpark in Bad Mergentheim**

<- *Wild animal park in Bad Mergentheim*

Weikersheim

Hier befand sich über Jahrhunderte die Residenz der einst mächtigen Grafen und Herren, später Fürsten von Hohenlohe. Den sehenswerten Ortskern ließen sie Anfang des 18. Jahrhunderts passend zu ihrem Schloss gestalten. Der **Marktplatz** wird im Osten von der spätgotischen Pfarrkirche (1419, Grabdenkmäler ab 15. Jh.) abgeschlossen und im Norden und Süden von barocken Amtshäusern flankiert. Daran schließen sich halbkreisförmig die niedrigen Zirkelhäuser an, einst Wohnung für Schlossbedienstete, die in der Mitte den Zugang zum

Weikersheim

For centuries, this was the residence of the once mighty Counts and Lords, later Princes, of Hohenlohe. The centre of the village is worth seeing; they had it adapted in the early 18th century to suit the style of their palace. The **market square** ends on its east side in the later Gothic parish church (1419, tombs dating from the 15th century onwards), flanked on the north and south sides by baroque houses once occupied by Court officials, and leaving space in the middle for access to the **palatial complex** and its main entrance. It is well worth looking

Blick über den Marktplatz auf die Zufahrt zum Schloss

Two pituresque quadrant houses flank the entrance to the palace

Schlosskomplex und seinem Haupteingang freilassen. Eine Besichtigung wert sind die vollständig erhaltene, kostbare Einrichtung, meist aus dem 18. Jahrhundert, die prächtig stuckierten Wohnräume und besonders der **Rittersaal** im Südflügel. Er nimmt zwei Stockwerke des Renaissance-Baus (um 1600) ein und galt als einer der größten und schönsten seiner Zeit. Die mächtige Kassettendecke ist mit Ketten im Dachstuhl befestigt und mit lebendigen Jagdszenen bemalt. Wertvolle Gemälde sowie zahlreiche Landschaftsbilder, Ornamente und plastisch hervortretende kapitale Wildtiere zieren die

round the completely preserved and valuable interior, most of it dating from the 18th century, such as the magnificent stucco-work in the residential rooms and in particular the **Rittersaal** or Knights' Hall in the south wing. It takes up two storeys of the Renaissance building (about 1600) and was regarded as the largest and most beautiful of its day. The massive grid-pattern ceiling is suspended by chains from the roof trusses, and painted with realistic hunting scenes. Valuable portraits and numerous landscapes, ornaments, and three-dimensional heads of wild animals decorate the walls. Even more

Schloss Weikersheim: Der Rittersaal präsentiert sich noch heute in seiner prunkvollen Ausstattung

Weikersheim Castle: The hall of knights can still be seen today in the original magnificence

Der Schlossgarten mit Orangerie

The castle garden with the orangery

Der Schlossgarten lässt die Zeit des Barock wieder lebendig werden

The palace garden brings the baroque age back to life

Wände. Noch überwältigender wirken die prachtvollen Stuckaufbauten des Kamins und des Portals – mit dem Relief einer Türkenschlacht – an den Schmalseiten des Festsaals. Schloss Weikersheim ist Sitz der „Jeunesses Musicales Deutschland". Diese führt hier eine Musikakademie, eine der größten musikalischen Bildungsstätten Deutschlands. So ist das Schloss heute Treffpunkt für Kurse, Konzerte, Opernaufführungen und Kongresse von jungen Musikern aus aller Welt. Ein Spaziergang im **Schlossgarten** versetzt den Besucher in die Zeit des Barock zurück mit geometrisch angelegten Beeten und Wegen, einer Orangerie und Heerscharen von Statuen aus der Welt der Antike und des Hoflebens im 18. Jahrhundert.

Als Kontrapunkt zum höfischen Prunk zeigt das Tauberländer **Dorfmuseum** die eher bescheidenen Geräte und Einrichtungsgegenstände der einfachen Landbevölkerung. Vermittelnd zwischen beiden steht das **Forstmuseum** im Schlösschen Karlsberg (1736), das die Entwicklung aufzeigt von der höfischen Jagd aus der Zeit des Barock bis zur modernen Forstwirtschaft der Gegenwart.

Schloss Weikersheim, einst Residenz der Fürsten von Hohenlohe, vom Schlossgarten gesehen

Weikersheim Castle, once the residence of the Princes of Hohenlohe, seen from its gardens

overwhelming are the magnificent stucco structures around the fireplace and the entrance doorway, including a bas-relief representation of a battle with the Turks, on the short wall of the banqueting hall. Parts of this palace house an off-shoot of the Württemberg State Museum. Every year the young musicians of Musikalische Jugend Deutschlands meet here for courses, concerts, and performances of operas with international singers. A wall through the **gardens of the palace** takes the visitor back through time to the baroque age, with their geometrically arranged flower-beds and paths, an orangery, and regiments of statues from antique times and from Court life in the 18th century.

As a counter-point to the courtly pomp, the Tauberland **Village Museum** shows the more modest implements and equipment of the simple country people, and as a mediator between the two there is the **Forestry Museum** in the Schlösschen or mini-palace up on the Karlsberg (1736), showing the historical development.

Blick von der Schlosseinfahrt gegen die spätgotische Pfarrkirche

View from the entrance of the palace to the late Gothic parish church

Röttingen

Der Weinort Röttingen (1800 Einwohner) liegt an der Einmündung des Rippbachs in die Tauber. 1953 zur ersten Europastadt überhaupt gekürt, gefällt Röttingen durch seinen historischen Ortskern mit malerischen Bildstöcken und anmutigen Fachwerkhäusern rund um das von stolzem Bürgersinn zeugende barocke Rathaus. Hier am **Marktplatz** beginnt und endet der etwa 1,5 km lange **„Sonnenuhrenweg"** mit etwa 25 dieser heute ungewöhnlichen Zeitmesser. An längst vergangene Zeiten erinnert auch die romanische **Pfarrkirche St. Kilian**, in deren Innerem noch Grabdenkmäler aus dem 13. Jahrhundert erhalten sind. Die sagenumwobene **Burg Brattenstein** ist heute renoviert und bildet in der warmen Jahreszeit die Kulisse für das bekannte Freilichttheater. Vielfältige Freizeiteinrichtungen und hübsche Parkanlagen bieten dem Gast eine hohe Urlaubsqualität in schöner Umgebung inmitten von Wäldern und Weinbergen.

Sonnenuhr in der Altstadt

Röttingen

The little wine-making village of Röttingen (population: 1,800) lies at the confluence of the Rippbach and the Tauber. It was elected in 1953 to be the first ever European Town, and appeals to the visitor because of its historic town centre with picturesque carvings and graceful half-timbered buildings all around a baroque town hall that bursts with civic pride. The Sonnenuhrweg or „sun-dial route", about 1,5 kilometres long, starts and finishes in this **market square**, passing some 25 of these now rare time instruments. The Roman-style **parish church** of St. Kilian also commemorates dim and distant days; its interior still preserves tombs dating from the 13th century. The fabled **castle of Brattenstein** has now been renovated, and during the warmer months forms the backdrop for the well-known open-air theatre. The visitor is offered a high quality of holiday with a wide range of leisure facilities and attractive parks and gardens, all in the lovely setting of forests and vineyards.

Sundial in the old Town

Creglingen

Creglingen besitzt seit 1349 Stadtrechte, die ihr vom damaligen Kaiser Karl IV. verliehen wurden. Drei Türme der einstigen Stadtmauer sind dort erhalten. Einen Besuch wert sind auch das **Lindleinturm-Museum** und das **Jüdische Museum**.

Berühmt wurde der Ort durch das schönste Schnitzwerk Tilman Riemenschneiders, das in der **Herrgottskirche** – 2 km außerhalb im Herrgottstal – untergebracht ist. Das Gotteshaus ließen sich die Herren von Hohenlohe-Brauneck 1386-89 erbauen, nachdem der Legende nach ein Bauer an dieser Stelle beim Pflügen eine Hostie gefunden hatte. Um 1500 schmückten es ihre Nachfolger mit bedeutenden Kunstwerken aus, darunter auch dem genannten **Marienaltar** (1505-10). Nachdem die Kirche 1530 evangelisch geworden war, schloss man den Altar und behängte ihn mit Totenkränzen. Er geriet in Vergessenheit und blieb bis zur Wiedereröffnung 1832 über drei Jahrhunderte unverändert. 11 m hoch erhebt

Creglingen

Creglingen became a free imperial city in 1349 thanks to emperor Charles IV. Three towers of the former town wall are still preserved. You shouldn't miss the **Lindleinturm Museum** and the **Jewish Museum**.

Creglingen became famous for the most beautiful of all Tilman Riemenschneider's carvings, which is to be found in the **Herrgottskirche**, 2 kilometres to the south in Herrgott valley. The lords of Hohenlohe-Brauneck built the church in 1386 – 89, after a peasant, as legend relates, had found the Host here while ploughing. In about 1500 their successors decorated it with major works of art including the **Altar to the Virgin Mary** (1505-10), already mentioned. After the church had become evangelical in 1530, the altar was closed and garlanded with wreathes. It fell into oblivion, and it remained unchanged for more than three centuries until it was re-opened in 1832. This masterpiece is 11 metres high and the shrine is made of reddish pinewood whe-

Partie an der Tauber   *Section of the Tauber*

Marienaltar von Tilman Riemenschneider

Tilman Riemenschneider: the altar of the Virgin Mary

sich das Meisterwerk, dessen Schrein aus rötlichem Kiefernholz gefertigt ist. Die Figuren sind aus hellem Lindenholz und beeindrucken durch den edlen Fluss der Gewandfalten und Haarpracht, die zartgliedrigen Hände und die ergreifenden Gesichter. Ein weiteres bedeutendes Meisterwerk in der Herrgottskirche ist der Altar im Chor, der aus der Schule des berühmten Veit Stoß stammen soll, und gefällige Bilder vermutlich von Michael Wolgemut, dem Lehrmeister Albrecht Dürers, enthält. Der Kirche gegenüber liegt das Fingerhutmuseum mit 3500 Exponaten. Fingerhüte waren in der Vergangenheit nicht nur Arbeitsgegenstand, sondern auch Edelschmuck.

reas its figures are made of light-coloured lindenwood. It impresses because of the splendid flow of the folds in the garments and the magnificent hair decoration, the delicately sculptured hands and the moving faces. Other masterpieces in Herrgott Church are the altar of the choir, possibly made by the school of the famous Veit Stoss, and the fine paintings probably by Michael Wolgemut, Albrecht Dürer's teacher. In front of the Herrgottskirche you can visit the Thimble Museum with 3500 exhibits. In the past, thimbles were not only instruments of work but also pieces of jewellery.

Herrgottskirche
Christ church

**Fingerhutmuseum:
Kunstreiche
Fingerhütte**

*Thimble museum:
Artistic thimbles*

Rothenburg
ob der Tauber

Über dem Tal erhebt sich im Schnittpunkt von Romantischer und Burgenstraße die unvergleichliche Silhouette der ehemaligen Reichsstadt. Vor allem im 30-jährigen Krieg verarmt und bedeutungslos geworden, blieb das altfränkische Stadtbild des Mittelalters samt der Turm bewehrten Befestigungsmauer über Jahrhunderte unversehrt erhalten.

Die Westseite des historischen Marktplatzes bildet der Volutengiebel der **Ratsherrntrinkstube** (1446) mit einer Sonnenuhr und der Stadtuhr (1683). In den seit-

Rothenburg
ob der Tauber

Above the valley, at the point where the Romantic Road and the Castles Road intersect, towers the incomparable silhouette of the former Imperial City. Reduced to poverty and insignificance mainly by the Thirty Years War, the medieval appearance of the old Franconian town, complete with its encircling wall and defensive towers, remained unchanged for centuries.

On the Maktplatz, the western side of the historic square is formed by the soaring gable of the **Ratsherrntrinkstube** or Councillors' drinking-room (1446), with a sun-

lichen Butzenfenstern erscheinen zwischen 11 und 15 sowie zwischen 20 und 22 Uhr jeweils zur vollen Stunde die Hauptfiguren des „Meistertrunks", der nach der Überlieferung im Jahr 1631 die Stadt vor der Zerstörung rettete. Die Südseite bildet das prächtige **Rathaus**, das seinen Renaissancebau (1572-78, Arkadenanbau 1681) dem Platz zuwendet. An den alten, vom Brand des Jahres 1501 unversehrt gebliebenen Bau erinnert noch heute der gotische Westbau mit dem schlanken Glockenturm, von dem man eine einzigartige Aussicht hat. Die Historiengewölbe mit dem Verließ sind eine Besichtigung wert. Ein unvergleichliches Ensemble bilden an der Turmseite des Rathauses der hübsche

dial and the town clock (1683). The small windows at the side open every hour on the hour to show the main figures involved in the Meistertrunk; according to tradition, this was a magic potion which the fighting men of the town drank in 1631 before storming out against a besieging army and thus saved the town from destruction. The south side is formed by the magnificent **Rathaus**, or town hall, with its Renaissance building (1572-78, arcades added 1681) turned towards the square. The Gothic western part of the building with the slender clock-towers, which survived the great fire of 1501 unscathed, still today serves as a reminder of the old town hall. There is an incomparable architectural group on the

Der Marktplatz mit dem Renaissance-Rathaus

The market square with the Renaissance town hall

Der St. Georgs- oder Herterichsbrunnen

St. George's- or Herterich fountain

Die Kunstuhr am Giebel der Ratsherrntrinkstube

The artistic clock of the Ratsherrntrinkstube

Rothenburgs Hauptkirche St. Jakob

Gemälde des Herlin-Altars

Painting of the Herlin Altar

Rothenburg's main church St. Jacob

Herlin-Altar: Stadtansicht von 1501

Herlin Altar: The city in 1501

St. Georgs- oder Herterichsbrunnen (1608) mit den Fachwerkgiebeln des ehemaligen Fleisch- und Tanzhauses (13. Jh.) und des Jagstheimerhauses (1488), heute Marien-Apotheke. Mit seinem malerischen Erker über einer Heiligenfigur und seinem stimmungsvollen Innenhof zählt das Gebäude zu den schönsten Patrizierhäusern Rothenburgs. Im Innern der gotischen Hauptkirche St. Jakob sind zwei Ausstattungstücke besonders bemerkenswert: der farbenprächtige, vergoldete **Hauptaltar** mit meisterlichen Gemäldetafeln von Friedrich Herlin (1466) – darunter eine Darstellung des Rothenburger Marktplatzes aus jener Zeit – sowie der **Heiligblutaltar** auf der Westempore. Es handelt sich dabei um ein imponierendes Schnitzwerk Riemenschneiders mit einer Darstellung des Abendmahls. Beim malerischen Feuerleinserker (um 1600) betreten wir den Hof des ehemaligen **Dominikanerinnenklosters** (13. Jh.), dessen historische Räume heute das **Reichsstadtmuseum** beherbergen. Hier blieben neben anderen Wohn-, Schlaf- und Wirtschaftsräumen auch die Kräuter- und die Klosterküche (um 1300) erhalten, wohl die älteste Küche Deutschlands. Zum Klingenturm (13. Jh.) mit sei-

tower side of the town hall, consisting of the attractive fountain called either **St George's or the Herterichsbrunnen** (1608), with the half-timbered gable wall of the former Fleisch- und Tanzhaus, a butchers' guild hall also used for dancing and revelry (13th century), and the Jagstheimerhaus (1488), once the home of a wealthy merchant and now housing a traditional pharmacy, the Marienapotheke. With its picturesque oriole window above a statue of a saint, the building is one of the finest patrician houses in Rothenburg. The town's **principal church, the Gothic Jakobskirche** (1311-1484). In the interior of the Jakobskirche, with its innumerable wealth of works of art, two items are particularly worth looking it: the brilliantly colourful, gilded **High Altar**, with magnificent painted panels by Friedrich Herlin (1466), and beneath it a representation of the market square of Rothenburg at that time, and the **Altar of the Holy Blood** on the western altar steps. This is one of the most impressive works of the carver Riemenschneider, and depicts the Last Supper. The picturesque Feuerleinserker ,(an oriole window, about 1600) the courtyard of the former **Dominican cloister** (13th century), and

Jakobskirche: der Heiligblutaltar des berühmten Holzschnitzers Tilman Riemenschneider

Jakobs church: The Altar of the Holy Blood by the famous wood-carver Tilman Riemenschneider

ner Bastei (1500), gehörte die turmlose **St.-Wolfgangs-Kirche**. Sie diente der Landbevölkerung, vor allem den Schäfern, als Gotteshaus, der Stadt jedoch ebenso als Wehrbau. In ihrem Innern sind neben den ansprechenden Altären deshalb auch die Wehranlagen beachtenswert: der Aufgang zum äußeren Torturm (heute Schäfertanz-Kabinett), von dort der Wehrgang in der Nordwand mit seiner Verbindung zum angrenzenden Geschützboden und die Kasematten, die unterhalb des Kirchenbodens eingebaut sind. Im **Burggarten** standen einst die Grafenburg (um 1000) und die Reichsburg (12. Jh.), beide 1356 durch ein Erdbeben zerstört. Die Gartenanlage, der Ausblick ins Tal und entlang der Stadtmauer nach Süden sowie die **Blasiuskapelle**, erbaut um 1400 aus Resten des Palas der Reichsburg sowie das Wappen

Das wappengeschmückte Burgtor mit dem malerischen Torhäuschen

The decorated coat of arms gate with the pictuesque building

the historical rooms of the **Reichstadtmuseum**, the museum depicting the town's history as an Imperial City. A number of living rooms, bedrooms, stores, and suchlike have been preserved, including the herbal and monastery kitchen (about 1300), which must now be the oldest kitchen in Germany. The **Klingenturm** (13th century),belonging to **St Wolfgang's church**, which had no tower of its own. Accordingly, in the interior there is not only a fine altar but also defensive buildings; the steps up to the outer gateway tower (now called the Schäfertanz-Kabinett, or shepherds' dancing-room) provide access to the fortifications of the north wall, which is then connected to the gun emplacements and casemates built in below the floor of the church. The **Burggarten** or castle garden, where once the old castles,

Blick von der St.-Wolfgangs-Kirche auf den Klingenturm

View from St. Wolfgang's church and the Klingen tower

Die Herrngasse mit dem hübschen Herrnbrunnen

The Herrngasse with the Herrnbrunnen fountain

geschmückte Burgtor (14. Jh.) lassen einen Besuch der Anlage dennoch lohnenswert erscheinen.Der Stadtteil Detwang, älter als Rothenburg, ist bekannt durch seine stimmungsvolle romanische Kirche (um 970, in gotischer Zeit verändert) mit dem herrlichen Kreuzaltar, den Tilman Riemenschneider (1460-1531) anfertigte. Nicht weit davon steht der Wohnturm „Topplerschlösschen"(1388), einst Sommersitz des berühmtesten Rothenburger Bürgermeisters und heute zu besichtigen.

Die **Herrngasse wird** gesäumt von prächtigen Patrizierhäusern mit romantischen Innenhöfen (Nr. 18,15,13,11). Rechts erhebt sich die **Franziskanerkirche** (um 1300), in der neben dem bemalten Lettner kunstvolle Epitaphien und der Franziskusaltar (Riemenschneider) erhalten sind. Hinter dem Herrnbrunnen befindet sich das sehenswerte Deutsche Weihnachtsmuseum. Am Beginn der Schmiedgasse begrüßt uns die hübsche Renaissance-Fassade des **Baumeisterhauses** mit einer Darstellung der 7 Tugenden und 7 Laster. In der Schmiedgasse wird die Entwicklung von Rothenburgs Altstadt besonders deutlich. An der Johanniskirche ist noch heute die Türangel des südlichen

the Grafenburg (about 1000) and the Reichsburg (12th century) used to stand until they were both destroyed in an earthquake in 1356.It is worthwhile to visit the gardens on account of the view out over the valley and along the town wall to the south, and to see St Blasius' chapel, built in 1400. The outlying village of Detwang is older than Rothenburg, it is well known for its charming Roman-style church (about 1170, renovated in Gothic times) with its magnificent cross altar produced by Tilman Riemenschneider (1460-1531). Not far away is a tower-like house, the Töpplerschlösschen or „Töppler's little castle" (1388) – once the summer residence of Rothenburg's most famous mayor, and nowadays open to the public. The **Herrngasse**, lined on either side by magnificent patrician houses with romantic internal courtyards (Nos. 18, 15, 13, and 11). On the right we can see the Franciscan church (about 1300), which contains not only the painted rood screen but also artistic epitaphs and the Altar of St Francis (Tilman Riemenschneider). Passing a fine fountain, the Herrnbrunnen, we reach the picturesque Hofbronnengasse opposite the town

Das Plönlein mit Blick auf den Siebersturm (links) und den Kobollzeller Turm

The Plönlein with view to the Siebersturm (left) and the Kobolzeller Turm

Stadttors (12. Jh.) zu sehen. Links markiert der „Alte Stadtgraben" den Mauerverlauf. Rechts befindet sich in den Gebäuden des ehemaligen Johanniterordens das reich ausgestattete **Mittelalterliche Kriminalmuseum**, Deutschlands bedeutendstes Rechtskundemuseum. Einige Meter weiter südwärts sehen wir vom **Plönlein** aus gleich zwei Stadttore, die bei der ersten Stadterweiterung (ab 1204) entstanden: das wehrhafte Kobolzeller Tor mit Bastei an der Talzufahrt – unterhalb überspannt die **Doppelbrücke** seit 1330 die Tauber.

Im Innenhof des **Spitals** steht das hübsche Hegereiterhaus. In der Rödergasse gefallen das mächtige Rödertor mit Bastei sowie der zierliche **Röderbogen** (mit Dachreiter) mit dem mächtigen **Markusturm**, flankiert von prächtigen Bürgerhäusern. Das Alt-Rothenburger Handwerkerhaus blieb seit seiner Bauzeit (13. Jh.) weitgehend unverändert, und seine Wohnräume und Werkstätten sind im Stil vergangener Jahrhunderte eingerichtet. Hinter dem Röderbogen lehnt sich rechts das Büttelhaus, einst Stadtgefängnis, an den Markusturm an. Nahe dem Kapellenplatz steht der **Weiße Turm** mit dem "Judentanzhaus".

Das wappengeschmückte Kobollzeller Tor war Stadtzufahrt aus dem Taubergrund

The Kobollzell Bastion with its coats of arms

Röderbogen mit „Osterschmuck" am Röderbrun-nen

The Röder Arch with „easter decorated" Röder fountain

hall, where we can visit a **dolls and toys museum**. At the Schmiedgasse, we are greeted by the attractive Renaissance façade of the **Baumeisterhaus**, with its depiction of the Seven Virtues and the Seven Deadly Sins. The hinges of the old south gate of the town (12th century) can still be seen today on the Johanniskirche, and on the left the street called Alter Stadtgraben marks the former line of the town wall. On the right, in the building which once housed the Order of St John, is the well-stocked **Medieval Criminology Museum**, the most important museum in Germany for forensic science. A few metres further southwards, from **Plönlein**, we can see two town gates at once which were built when the town was extended in 1204; the defensive gate of the Kobolzeller Tor with its barbican leading down into the valley where, far below it, the double bridge has spanned the Tauber since 1330.

The **Röderbogen** archway with its ridge turrets, the massive **tower of St Mark's** flanked by magnificent patrician houses, and, in the foreground, the fine Rö-derbrunnen fountain. Behind the Röderbogen, on its right, the old town prison Büttelhaus leans up against St Mark's church.

Das Rödertor   *The Röder Gate*

Alte Schmiede
The old forge

Schillingsfürst

Das Residenzstädtchen Schillingsfürst wird überragt vom mächtigen **Barockschloss** der Fürsten von Hohenlohe-Schillingsfürst. 365 Fenster spenden den 70 Räumen Licht. Reiches Stuckwerk, kunstvolle Deckengemälde und Gobelins, auserlesene Möbel, feines Porzellan und kostbare Bilder erwecken die Geschichte des 18. und 19. Jahrhunderts zu neuem Leben. Das Arbeitszimmer des Reichskanzlers Chlodwig enthält noch die Originaleinrichtung aus der Zeit um 1900. Das Schloss zeigt seinen Besuchern ein Museum mit kostbarem Interieur und liebenswerten Details.

An dieser exponierten Stelle hatte es bereits um das Jahr 1000 eine mächtige Burg gegeben, die mehrmals zerstört wurde. Zwischen 1723 und 1750 entstand der heutige Komplex als Residenzschloss des Hohenloher Fürstenhauses. Von hier oben hat man einen herrlichen Rundblick über die Frankenhöhe, die Hohenloher Ebene und den Ort. Hier hat der Bayerische Jagdfalkenhof seinen Sitz. Die zahlreichen dressierten **Greifvögel** bekommen bei schönem Wetter auch den nötigen Aufwind für ihr tägliches Flugtraining und Schaufliegen. Das „**Brunnenhausmuseum**" wird überragt von einem Wasserturm. Einmalig ist die Art der Pumpanlage im Brunnenhaus, die „Ochsentretanlage" (1704) der fürstlichen Wasserversorgung.

Schloss Schillingsfürst

Schillingsfürst

The small town of Schillingsfürst, nestling beneath the imposing **baroque mansion** of the Princes of Hohenlohe- Schillingsfürst. It boasts 70 rooms, lit by 365 windows. Rich stucco work, artistic ceiling paintings and tapestries, lovingly selected furniture, fine porcelain and valuable portraits bring the 18th and 19th centuries back to life. The study of Chancellor Chlodwig, a successor of Bismarck as Chancellor of the German Empire, still contains its original furniture dating from around 1900. The palace invites the visitor to see a museum with a priceless interior and loving details.

There had already been a massive castle at this exposed position in the Year 1000, but this was destroyed on a number of occasions. The present complex of buildings came into being between 1723 and 1750, as the residential palace of the princely house of Hohenlohe. From up here one has a magnificent view all around and across the Frankenhöhe hills, the Hohenlohe plain, and the little town, and here the numerous, highly trained hawks of the Bavarian **Falconry Centre** can find sufficient up-draught for their daily flight training and demonstration flights. The **Brunnenhausmuseum**, a solitary house overshadowed by an old water-tower.

Schillingsfürst castle

Schloss Schillingsfürst: Roter Salon

Schillingsfürst castle: Red Saloon

Gobelinsaal

Tapestry Saloon

Feuchtwangen

Die Siedlung entstand einst um ein im 8. Jahrhundert gegründetes Benediktinerkloster. Sie war seit dem 12. Jahrhundert bis 1376 freie Reichsstadt, als sie an die Markgrafschaft Brandenburg-Ansbach fiel. Seit 1806 gehört die Stadt mit nunmehr gut 12.000 Einwohnern zu Bayern.

In seltener Harmonie und Geschlossenheit präsentiert sich der **Marktplatz**, den man deshalb auch als „Frankens Festsaal" bezeichnet. Stolze Bürgerhäuser, heute meist im Dienst der Gastronomie, und das prächtige **Alte Rathaus** säumen den lang gezogenen Platz. Seinen nördlichen Abschluss bildet die gotische **Stiftskirche** (13./14. Jh.), Nachfolgebau der romanischen Klosterkirche St. Salvator. Sie hatte ursprünglich zum bereits erwähnten Benediktinerkloster gehört, das jedoch um 1150 in ein Chorherrenstift umgewandelt worden war. Seit 1623 dient die Stiftskirche als Feuchtwangens evangelisch-lutherische Hauptkirche. In ihrem Innern verdienen der Hochaltar, gemalt 1483 von Dürers Lehrmeister Michael Wolgemut aus Nürnberg, die Schnitzereien des Chorgestühls (um 1500) sowie das Grabmal des Stiftsherrn Lucas Freyer (1523) besondere Beachtung. Südlich an die Stiftskirche schließt sich der spätromanische **Kreuzgang** an, der noch aus der Zeit des Benediktinerklosters stammt. Im Obergeschoss über dem Westflügel sind in den „Handwerkerstuben" sechs Originalwerkstätten – Zuckerbäcker, Färber, Zinngießer, Hafner, Schuster und Weber – eingerichtet. Alljährlich in den Sommermonaten finden im Innenhof die bekannten Kreuzgangspiele als Freilichttheater statt.

Den barocken **Röhrenbrunnen** (1727) am Marktplatz zieren neben der Figur auf der Brunnensäule farbige Wappentafeln. Gleich beim Brunnen beginnt die romantische Museumsgasse mit ihren historischen oder stilechten Giebelhäusern. Fast am Ende der Straße weisen eine hölzerne Pumpanlage und ein steinerner Geldzähltisch auf das **Fränkische Museum** hin, das in einem Bau von 1789 untergebracht ist. Innen sind bürgerliche Stubeneinrichtungen aus den Stilrichtungen von Barock bis Jugendstil zu besichtigen, besonders aber eine qualitätvolle Sammlung von Fayencen. Der neuzeitliche Anbau des Museums steht auf dem Platz einer Synagoge von 1833, die 1938 dem Rassenwahn zum Opfer fiel. Dem mittelalterlichen Minnesänger Walther von der Vogelweide (um 1200) und seiner Lyrik ist der Brunnen gegenüber gewidmet, der Geschichte des fränkischen Sängerbundes das nahe Fränkische Sängermuseum (seit 1989).

Feuchtwangen

The town originally developed around a Benedictine monastery founded in the 8th century. From some time in the 12th century until 1376 it was a Free Imperial City, but was then ceded to the Counts of Brandenburg-Ansbach, and since 1806 has belonged to Bavaria.

The **Marktplatz** (Market Square) presents a rare spectacle of harmony and completeness which has earned it the name of „Franconia's Festival Hall". Proud patrician houses, most of them nowadays devoted to the hotel and catering trade, and the magnificent **Altes Rathaus** line the edges of the long, narrow Platz. It had originally belonged to the Benedictine monaster, but was converted in 1150 to a Chorherrenstift, a church with a choir under the patronage of the local aristocracy. It has served since 1623 as the main Evangelical-Lutheran church of Feuchtwangen. Inside, the High Altar, painted in 1483 by Michael Wolgemut, the master who taught Dürer, the carvings on the Choir stool (about 1500), and the tomb of the monastery's patron Lucas Freyer (1523) deserve particular attention. On the south side of the monastery church is the late-Roman style **cloister**, dating right back to the time of the Benedictine monastery. In the upper storey, above the west wing, there are six original workshops in the „Craftsmen's rooms": a sugar-baker, a dyer, a pewter-caster, a potter, a cobbler, and a weaver. Every year, during the summer months, the well-known Cloister Plays take place, using the inner courtyard as an open-air theatre.

The baroque fountain on the south, the **Röhrenbrunnen** (1727), is decorated not only with the figure on the column but also by a colourful genealogy illustrated with coats-ofarms. The Museumsgasse starts just alongside the fountain, and is full of gabled houses which are either historically genuine or authentically restored. Almost at the far end of the street, a wooden pump and a stone money- counter mark the **Franconian Museum**, housed in a building dating from 1789. Inside, room-settings showing townspeople's lives from the baroque to the Art Nouveau ages can be seen, and in particular a very fine collection of faience ware. The modern extension to the museum building occupies the earlier site of a synagogue, built in 1833 and destroyed in the wave of racial hatred in 1938. The fountain opposite is dedicated to the medieval bard, Walther von der Vogelweide (about 1200) and his poetry, and the nearby **Franconian Singers' Museum** to the history of the Franconian Singers' Association (since 1989).

Szene der Kreuzgang Spiele ->

Scene from the Cloisters Plays ->

Marktplatz mit Barockbrunnen und spätgotischer Stiftskirche

The market square with the baroque fountain

Spätromanischer Kreuzgang und Bayrische Spielbank Feuchtwangen

Late roman cross coat and the Bavarian Casino

Dinkelsbühl

Die ursprüngliche Ansiedlung entstand aus einem fränkischen Königshof und wurde bereits vor der Jahrtausendwende zur Sicherung der sich hier kreuzenden Handelswege Ostsee-Italien und Worms-Prag befestigt. An dieser Kreuzung erhebt sich das spätgotische **Münster St. Georg** (1448-99), bei dem das Missverhältnis zwischen dem mächtigen Langhaus einerseits und dem trotz seiner 62 m Höhe recht niedrig wirkenden Turm andererseits ins Auge fällt. Das kommt daher, dass der heutige Turm um 1225 für die kleinere romanische Vorgängerkirche gebaut worden war, vom geplanten gotischen Kirchturm an der Nordflanke jedoch aus wirtschaftlichen Gründen lediglich das Erdgeschoss aufgeführt wurde, das als Sakristei dient. Dafür entstand das Langhaus unter den Kirchenbaumeistern Nikolaus Eseler, Vater und Sohn, in nur 51 Jahren Bauzeit „aus einem Guss", so dass St. Georg heute als schönste Hallenkirche Süddeutschlands gilt.

Gegenüber dem romanischen Turmportal beginnt die Segringer Straße. Auf ihrer linken Seite fällt das **He-**

Blick von der Segringer Straße auf das Münster St. Georg

Dinkelsbühl

The original settlement arose as the Court of a Frankish king, and was fortified before the start of our millennium as a place of refuge on the trading routes, from the Baltic to Italy and from Worms to Prague, that intersected here. It was at this cross-roads that the late Gothic **St George's church** arose (1448-99), which strikes the eye because of its false proportions: the nave on the one hand is too high and the tower on other hand, despite being 62 metres tall, still seems very low. This is due to the fact that the tower we see today was built about 1225 for the earlier church on this site, a smaller one in the Roman style. A Gothic church tower was planned for the north flank, but for economic reasons only the ground floor, which now serves as a vestry, was built. On the other hand, the nave was built by the master builders of churches, Nikolaus Eseler father and son, in only 51 years and all as one complete unit, so that St George's is now regarded as the most beautiful church of its type in southern Germany. On the left-hand side the eye catches the **Hezelhaus** with its fine half-timbered facade

View of the Segringer Street to the St. George's church

elhaus mit seiner schmucken Fachwerkfassade und em vorspringenden Giebel ins Auge. Besondere Bechtung verdient dabei der verträumte Innenhof, der den Besucher in die Zeit des Mittelalters zurückversetzt. Rechts der Segringer Straße beginnt mit der Türmchen ekrönten Ratstrinkstube (um 1600) eine besonders harmonische Häuserreihe, aus welcher der reich verzierte Fachwerkbau „Deutsches Haus" und die wuchtige Giebelfront der Schranne herausragen. Dort beginnt ie Dr.-Martin- Luther-Straße, die zum Rothenburger Tor führt. Kurz davor liegt rechts der Spitalkomplex gestiftet 1280, heutige Gebäude 15./16. Jh.), heute .a. Altersheim und Historisches Museum. Chor und akristei der Spitalkirche stammen noch aus dem 14. ahrhundert.

and projecting gable wall. The dreamy inner courtyard deserves particular attention, as it takes the visitor straight back to the Middle Ages. On the right-hand side of the Segringer Strasse, a particularly harmonious row of houses starts with the turreted Ratstrinkstube (the town councillor's drinking-room, about 1600), the other outstanding examples being the richly decorated, half-timbered Deutsches Haus and the powerful gable façade of the Schranne. This is where Dr Martin Luther Strasse starts, leading to the northern town gate, the Rothenburger Tor. Just before we reach that we will see the complex of buildings of the Spital, an infirmary endowed in 1280 (the present-day buildings date from the 15th and 16th centuries). Today they include an old-people's home and a museum of local arts and crafts.

Dinkelsbühl: Prächtige Giebelhäuser am Wein-markt, in der Mitte das „Deutsche Haus"

Dinkelsbühl: gorgeous gable houses at the Weinmarkt, in the middle the „Deutsches Haus"

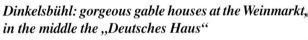

Gaulweiher mit Faulturm und Vorwerkhäuschen

Gaulweiher with the Faulturm and Vorwerkhäus-chen

Turmparade an der Stadtmauer

Tower parade at the city wall

Ein besonders malerischer Blick auf das Wappen geschmückte **Rothenburger Tor** (um 1390) mit seinem Vorwerk ergibt sich von der Außenseite über den **Gaulweiher** hinweg. Am Ende des Weihers präsentiert sich der runde Faulturm mit einem romantischen Vorwerkhäuschen. Die Weiher um die Stadt beherbergen übrigens Dinkelsbühls Spezialität, die Karpfen, was den Bewohnern schon früh den Spitznamen „Blausieder" einbrachte.

Die Promenade durch den gepflegten Park führt vorbei am mächtigen Grünen Turm zum Segringer Tor und weiter, vorbei an nicht weniger als acht Wehrtürmen, zum **Nördlinger Tor** (14. Jh., Giebel um 1600). Von aussen betrachtet, gefällt dabei der romantische **Bäuerlinsturm** mit Fachwerkoberbau und Walmdach vor dem Hintergrund des Münsters St. Georg und den Altstadtdächern. Ebenso wehrhaft wie die Mauer präsentiert sich die massige **Stadtmühle** neben dem Nördlinger Tor. Sie entstand, nachdem Kaiser Karl IV. 1378 der Stadt das Privileg zum Betrieb zweier Mühlstätten verliehen hatte. Da sie außerhalb der Stadtmauer lag, ließ man sie

The choir and the vestry of the Spitalkirche still date from the 14th century.

There is one particularly picturesque view of the **Rothenburger Tor** (about 1390), covered with its colourful coats-of-arms. The outside of the Spitalkirche across the **Gaulweiher** pond. At the end of the pond is another tower, the Faulturm, with romantic outbuildings.

A walk through the neatly tended park leads past the massive Grüner Turm to the Segringer Turm, and then on past no fewer than eight more defensive towers to the **Nördlinger Tor**. The particularly pleasing features are the **Bäuerlinsturm**, with its halftimbered superstructure and sloping roof, with St George's church and the higgledypiggledy roofs of the old town in the background. The massive **Stadtmühle**, or town mill, alongside the Nördlinger Tor, looks just as much like part of the defences as do the walls themselves. It was built in 1378, after the Emperor Karl IV had granted the town the privilege of operating two mills. The gable on the street side is the only part that was not built until about 1600. Just before the main church we encounter a baroque fountain and

Mühlgraben mit Bäuerlinsturm

Mill moat with Bäuerlins tower

Blick vom Altrathausplatz mit dem Löwenbrunnen auf das Wörnitztor

View of Wörnitztor from Altrathausplatz with lion fountain

mit Wehrgang und Schießscharten bis über die Radstatt und wehrhaften Rundtürmchen ausstatten. Lediglich der frühbarocke Giebel zur Straße hin entstand erst um 1600. Hier befindet sich das Museum 3. Dimension. Von der Klostergasse aus können wir den **Innenhof** des um 1290 gegründeten Klosters besichtigen. Rundbogige Arkaden schützen wertvolle alte Grabtafeln aus dem 16. Jahrhundert vor Witterungseinflüssen. Zwei Darstellungen erinnern an den Dinkelbauern, welcher der Legende nach einst die Siedlung gegründet hat.

An der Nördlinger Straße mündet die Klostergasse in den **Ledermarkt** mit seinen historischen Giebelhäusern. Er wird beherrscht vom massigen Bau des **Alten Rathauses**. Bereits 1361 als Bürgerhaus entstanden,

the Evangelical church of St Paul (1840), the successor to the Carmelite church. From the Klostergasse we see the **interior courtyard** of the monastery, which was founded in 1290. Roundarched arcades shield priceless old 16thcentury gravestones from the worst of the weather. Two illustrations commemorate the growers of durum wheat („Dinkel") who, according to legend, founded the settlement of Dinkelsbühl.

At the Nördlinger Strasse the Klostergasse opens out into the **Ledermarkt** with its historic gabled houses. It is dominated by the massive structure of the **Altes Rathaus**, which was built as long ago as 1361 as the home of a wealthy citizen. It was made over to the town in the 16th century, which after making the necessary

Haus der Geschichte

House of history

kaufte es die Stadt im 16. Jahrhundert und nutzte es nach der notwendigen Erweiterung bis 1855 für ihr Stadtparlament. Heute ist hier das „Haus der Geschichte Dinkelsbühl, – von Krieg und Frieden –" untergebracht. Zentrum des Altrathausplatzes ist der Löwenbrunnen (16. Jh.), dessen Hauptfigur eine Wappentafel trägt, Gepflegte Giebelhäuser sowie das Wörnitztor bilden einen malerischen Hintergrund für den Brunnen wie für das genannte Festspiel, dessen zweiter Teil, die Stadtübergabe, jeweils hier aufgeführt wird.

extensions used it for its council meetings until 1855. Another point worth attention is the entrance hall of the Altes Rathaus with its heavy wood ceiling and spiral staircase (1548). The focal point of the Altrathausplatz is the Löwenbrunnen, a fountain featuring a lion holding a coat-of-arms. Neatly maintained gabled houses form, together with the Wörnitztor, a picturesque backdrop for the fountain and for the children's play, the second part of which is always given here.

Festspiel „Die Kinderzeche"   *Children's festival*

Wallerstein und Schloss Baldern

Mitten auf der breiten Hauptverkehrsstraße des Marktfleckens (3200 Einwohner) grüßt schon von weitem, gleich hinter der Pfarrkirche (1613), die schlanke Dreifaltigkeits- oder **Pestsäule**. Aus einem Sockel mit lateinischen Inschriften wächst der Obelisk zwischen den Gestalten der Pestheiligen Rochus, Sebastian und Antonius von Padua empor zum goldenen Strahlenkranz, der zusammen mit Engeln und Wolken den christlichen Himmel symbolisiert. An der Spitze thronen Gottvater und Christus, zusammen mit dem Heiligen Geist die Dreiheit bildend. Unter ihnen steht die Muttergottes, Fürbitterin der Bedrängten, die zur Königin des Himmels gekrönt wird. Die Säule entstand in den Jahren 1720-25.

Das Schloss Wallerstein, heute in Besitz des Fürstenhauses Oettingen-Wallerstein, hat eine lange und wechselvolle Geschichte aufzuweisen: Die ursprüngliche Burganlage ist im Hochmittelalter in staufischer Hand. Erstmals 1150 urkundlich erwähnt, kommt sie 1250 an die „oettingischen" Gaugrafen, deren einzelne Linien sich im Lauf der Zeiten mehrfach im Besitz abwechseln. Nach 1602 entsteht durch einen Erben des Grafen Wilhelm II. von Oettingen, Ernst I., eine eigene Linie Oettingen-Baldern, die fast 200 Jahre Bestand hat und dort oben residiert.

Im Laufe des 17. Jahrhunderts wandelt sich durch zahlreiche bauliche Veränderungen die Burg zu einem Schloss. Die Heirat von Graf Notger Wilhelm zu Oettingen-Baldern mit der Gräfin und Erbtochter des Besitzers des Hauses Sötern sowie die nachfolgende Ehe des Grafen Anton Wilhelm mit der Gräfin Johanna Eleonore von Schönborn, und deren stattliche finanzielle Mitgift, ermöglichen den vorzüglichen barocken Ausbau des Schlosses zu seiner jetzigen Gestalt.

Gleich das äußere Portal zeigt einen imposanten Aufbau und vermittelt mit seinem von kräftigen Atlanten getragene Gebälk den Eindruck einer großartigen Residenz. Er steigert sich mit dem Betreten der Schlosskapelle mit ihren drei Altären, den seitlichen Emporen und der von zartem Stuck überzogenen, barocken Raumschale. Schauend und staunend durchschreitet man anschließend die Flucht der Gemächer, den roten, den grünen, den gelben Salon, bewundert die wundervollen Zierformen des Stucks, die Schönheit des Mobiliars, die Öfen, Gemälde, Uhren, Vasen, Lüster, das geschmackvolle Ambiente insgesamt.

Wallerstein and Baldern Castle

A small market town with a population of 3,000, its slender Dreifaltigkeitssäule, a column dedicated the Holy Trinity and also called the Pestsäule, or **„plague column"**, stands immediately behind the parish church (1613) as if in the middle the main motor road and greets the visitor from afar. This obelisk stands on a plinth bearing Latin inscriptions, and rises upwards between the three saints entrusted with keeping plague away: St Rochus, St Sebastian, and St Anthony of Padua, to the golden halo which, together with angels and clouds, symbolises the Christian Heaven. At its peak, God the Father and God the Son sit in majesty, forming the Trinity together with the Holy Ghost. At their feet sits Mary the Mother of God as advocate of the oppressed, and is crowned Queen of Heaven. The column was built in 1722-25.

Castle Baldern, now in the posession of the Principality of Oettingen-Wallerstein, this castle has a long and variable history to show. The original fortress belonged in medieval time to the Staufers. When it first mentioned in records in 1150 it was pledged to the Oettingschen Gaugrafen in 1250. The counts of Oettingen whose lines in time often changed the property the outcome of this heir of the Count Wilhelm II of Oettingen. Ernst the I an own line of Oettingen Baldern which consisted almost 200 years and resided there.

In the 17 th century the composition turned into a castle after many constructural changes.

The marriage of the Earl Notger Wilhelm of Oettingen-Baldern to the Countess and heiress of the properties Sötern as also the next marriage of the Earl Anton Wilhelm to the Countess Johanna Eleonore von Schönborn and the superb financial marriage portion allowed the exquisite baroque dismantling of the castle to its present form.

Right away the external porch shows an monumental composition and mediates with its strong carrying corpus callosum the impression of an aureate Residence. The impression grows with entering the Castle chapel with its 3 Altars, the side Altars and the baroque room coated with delicate stucco. Looking and wondering subsequently one crosses the chambers, the red, the green and yellow saloon. One admires the wonderfull adornemet of the stucco, the elegance of the furniture, The stoves, paintings, clocks, vases, chandeliers, the aesthetic ambiente in all.

Pestsäule und Pfarrkirche in Wallerstein

Plague column and parish church in Wallerstein

Rechts oben:
Der Speisesaal

Upper Right:
The dining room

Rechts mitte:
Das Grafenzimmer

Middle right:
The counts room

**Schloss Baldern aus
der Vogelperspektive**

*Aerial view of
Baldern Castle*

Nördlingen

Bereits in römischer und alamannischer Zeit war das heutige Stadtgebiet besiedelt. Im Jahr 898 ist der karolingische Königshof „Nordilinga" bezeugt, 1219 die 10 Tage dauernde Pfingstmesse, eine der bedeutendsten Fernhandelsmessen Oberdeutschlands. Durch sie gelangte die Stadt zu einigem Wohlstand und zu politischer Bedeutung. Die Freie Reichsstadt (seit 1215) konnte es sich im 14. Jahrhundert leisten, die Wehrmauer beträchtlich zu erweitern, um die inzwischen gewachsenen Vorstädte einzubeziehen. Im Verlauf des 30-jährigen Kriegs verlor die Stadt sowohl die Hälfte ihrer Bevölkerung als auch ihre Wirtschaftskraft und Bedeutung. Erst 1939 erreichte die Einwohnerzahl wieder die Höhe von 1618, knapp 9000. So gab es danach im Laufe von 3 Jahrhunderten kaum bauliche Veränderungen. Der Mauerring samt seinen wehrhaften Türmen ist bis heute geschlossen erhalten und trägt zusammen mit zahlreichen anderen historischen Bauwerken dazu bei, Nördlingen zu einem Anziehungspunkt für Besucher aus aller Welt zu machen. Mittelpunkt der Altstadt ist der **Marktplatz** mit dem **Tanzhaus** und dem **Hohen Haus** (15.bzw 13 Jh.), einem neunstöckigen Wohnturm. Das Tanzhaus besitzt

Nördlingen

The area of the town was already settled in Roman and Allemanic times. „Nordlinga" is recorded in 898 as one of the Royal courts of the Carolinian monarchs, and in 1219 it held a Whit Fair that lasted for 10 days and made it one of the most important trade fairs of Upper Germany. This brought it economic and political power, and this can still be seen in its buildings, monuments, and works of art. As a Free Imperial City (from 1215 onwards) it could afford, in the 14th century, to extended its defensive walls considerably and to incorporate the foregate, which had by then grown much larger. During the course of the Thirty Years War the town lost not only half its population but also its economic power and importance. It was not until 1939 that the population regained the numbers it had had in 1618, just short of 9,000. Even the encircling walls and defensive towers have been preserved, and together with numerous other historic buildings contribute to making Nördlingen a magnetic centre for visitors from all over the world.The **Marktplatz** or market square, which contains the **Tanzhaus** and the **Hohes Haus**, both built in 15th century. The latter is a 9-storey warehouse, and the Tanzhaus

Historische Altstadt mit Brot- und Tanzhaus (links) und Rathaus (rechts)

Historical old city, with the bread and dancehouse (left) and city hall (right)

einen prächtigen Fachwerkgiebel, dessen drei Stockwerke jeweils weit vorkragen. Es diente hauptsächlich als Verkaufsplatz der Tuchhändler zu Messezeiten. Ein Standbild des Kaisers Maximilian I., eines Gönners der Stadt, ziert die schlichte Fassade gegen den Marktplatz. Auch das **Rathaus** wurde im 13. Jahrhundert als Messekaufhaus genützt, dient jedoch bereits seit 1382 als städtisches Rathaus und ist damit eines der ältesten in Deutschland. Eine prächtige Steinmetzarbeit stellt die Renaissance- Freitreppe samt ihrem Portal dar, die seit 1618 eine frühere hölzerne Aufgangstreppe des Gebäudes ersetzt. Ihr gegenüber steht das ehemalige Leihhaus, wo heute die Tourist-Information beheimatet ist. Das markante „**Klösterle**" entstand einst als Kirche des Barfüßerklosters. Nach der Reformation nutzte es die Stadt als Getreidespeicher, später als Lagerraum und heute als Stadtsaal bei größeren Veranstaltungen. Das schöne

possesses a magnificent half-timbered gable with three storeys, each of its three storeys protruding far out beyond the one below it. Its main purpose originally was as a market for the cloth-traders visiting the trade fair. A standing portrait of the Emperor Maximilian I, a patron of the town, decorates the otherwise plain façade facing the market square. The **Rathaus** or town hall on the opposite side was also built in the 13th century as a traders' market, but has been used as the town hall since as long ago as 1382, which makes it one of the oldest in Germany. The outside Renaissance staircase with its doorway is a magnificent sample of the mason's work; it replaced a wooden access staircase at the rear of the building in 1618. Opposite is the old Leihhaus, where the Tourist Office now resides. The striking building, the **Klösterle**, originally the monastery church for a barefooted order of monks. The beautiful main entrance door

Hauptportal stammt aus der Zeit des Umbaus (1586). Gegenüber steht das **Kaisheimer Haus**, 1278-1803 Kastenhaus des Reichsstiftes Kaisheim, später Landgericht und Bezirksamt, heute Amtsgericht. Am westlichen Ende der Gerbergasse steht der scheunenartige Bau des „Holzhofs", den die Stadt Nördlingen als **Rieskrater-Museum** eingerichtet hat. Es zeigt – auf sechs Räume aufgeteilt – die Entstehung des Rieskraters im Speziellen und den Verlauf von Impaktprozessen (Kraterbildungsprozesse) im Allgemeinen. Im ehemaligen Hospitalgebäude ist das **Stadtmuseum** untergebracht, das die Geschichte Nördlingens und des Rieses dokumentiert. Besonders beeindrucken in der Sammlung die Inszenierung der Ofnethöhle mit den mittelsteinzeitlichen Schädelnestern (ca. 6000 v.Chr.), der römische Flötenspieler aus der nahe gelegenen villa rustica von Holheim, das Zinnfigurendiorama der berühmten Schlacht bei Nördlingen (1634), sowie die spätgotischen Tafelgemälde Friedrich Herlins (15. Jh.) und Hans Schäufelins (16. Jh.).
Die Herrengasse mündet in den Weinmarkt ein, wo der **Maria-Holl-Brunnen** an die tapfere Kronenwirtin erinnert, die während der Hexenprozesse 1589-98 trotz 62 schwerer Folterungen nicht gestand und ihren Prozess überlebte. Diese Verfahren brachten insgesamt 35 Menschen in Nördlingen den unverdienten Tod.

Die repräsentative Fassade des „Klösterle"

The representive fassade the „Klösterle"

Der stattliche Bau des Bürgerheims gehörte einst zum städtischen Spital

The nobel building was once part of the city hospital

dates from the time when the building was converted in 1586. The white building opposite is the **Kaisheimer Haus**, which served from 1278 to 1803 as the main store for the Imperial monastery of Kaisheim, later becoming the county court and administrative headquarters, and is now once again the local courthouse. At the western end is a barn-like building, called the Holzhof, used today as the **Rieskrater Museum**. This collection is concerned with the meteor which collided with the Earth 15 million years ago and made the crater which is now the stretch of countryside called the Nördlingen Ries. The **municipal museum** is housed in one of these buildings, and documents the history of Nördlingen. Particularly impressive items in the collection include casts of the skull nests from the Often caves (about 11,000 BC), the flute-player from Roman times, the late Gothic Herlin altar, and the scenic display of pewter figures depicting the famous Battle of Nördlingen (1634).

The Herrngasse finals opens into the Weinmarkt, where a **fountain** commemorates a courageous innkeeper's wife, **Maria Holl**, who despite having been subjected to agonising torture 56 times refused to give in and thus survived her trial as a witch. This bigotry had already cost 35 innocent people their lives.

Rieskrater-Museum   *The Rieskrater Museum*

Partie vor dem Löpsinger Tor

The section in front of the Löpsinger Tor

Stadtmuseum   *City Museum*

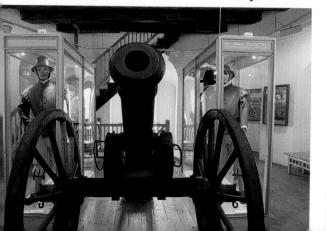

Das mächtige **Hallgebäude** (1543) diente einst als Speicher für Salz, Wein und Getreide. Die **Herrgotts- oder Salvatorkirche** war 1422 als Klosterkirche der Karmeliter geweiht worden. Die alte Bastei an der Stadtmauer dient heute als Freilichttheater. Die **St.-Georgs-Kirche** mit ihrem fast 90 m hohen Turm, dem „Daniel", ist nicht zu übersehen. Als eine der größten süddeutschen Hallenkirchen 1505 vollendet, bewahrt sie einen barocken Hochaltar mit spätgotischen Plastiken sowie einen spätgotischen Taufstein. Wer eine herrliche Aussicht über die Altstadt genießen will, der steige bei klarem Wetter die 350 Stufen hinauf zum Turmumgang. Von hier aus lässt der Türmer alle halbe Stunde von 22 bis 24 Uhr noch heute allnächtlich sein mittelalterliches Losungswort erschallen: „So, G'sell, so!" Beim Auf- und Abstieg begegnen wir dem alten Tretrad, mit dem der Türmer, Wächter über die Stadt und „Feuermelder", ein Seil mit Korb für seine Versorgung hinaufzog.

The massive **Hallgebäude** (1543) served as a warehouse for salt, wine, and grain. The Herrgottskirche or **St Salvator's church**, was consecrated in 1442 as the Carmelite's monastery church, but rather fundamentally altered in 1829. **St George's church**, its 90-metre tall tower, the „Daniel", dedicated in 1505 as one of the largest churches of its kind in southern Germany, it contains a baroque-style High Altar with late Gothic sculpture and altar panels and a late Gothic font. Anyone who would like a really good view out over the old town centre should choose a fine day and clamber the 350 stairs to the walkway round the top of the tower. From here, the watchman in the tower calls out his traditional medieval cry every half-hour, from 10.00 pm to midnight: „So, G'sell, so!" (very roughly: „All's well, fellows, all's well!"). Climbing and descending from the tower we encounter the old treadmill with which the watchmen and „fire warning" men pulled a basket up on a rope containing their nightly rations.

St. Georgs-Kirche mit mächtigem Turm, genannt „Daniel"

St. Georgs church with its mighty tower named „Daniel"

Der Turmwächter ruft vom „Daniel"

The tower keeper calls from the „Daniel"

St.-Georgs-Kirche: Langhaus gegen Westen   *St. Georg's Church: the nave*

Harburg

Das mittelalterliche Städtchen Harburg drängt sich an den steilen Hang zwischen der Wörnitz und dem Burgberg, auf dem die mächtige Burganlage thront. Als sie 1150 erstmals urkundlich erwähnt wurde, war sie noch im Besitz der staufischen Kaiser, erbaut zur Sicherung der Handelsstraße Augsburg-Nürnberg. 1251 und 1299 gelangten Stadt und Burg durch Verpfändung an die Grafen von Oettingen. Die Burg ist heute im Besitz der Gemeinnützigen Fürst zu Oettingen-Wallerstein-Kulturstiftung. Im Laufe ihrer langen Geschichte nie zerstört, gehört sie zu den besterhaltenen Burgen Deutschlands. Wegen der Enge des Raums ist die Romantische Straße in Höhe der **Burg** auf einer Länge von 300 m als Tunnel geführt. Davor steigt eine Straße rechts hinauf zum Parkplatz unterhalb der Burg, die durch hohe Mauern mit Wehrgängen und eine doppelte Toranlage gesichert war. Am inneren Tor ist noch das hölzerne Fallgatter mit seinen eisernen Spitzen erhalten. Um den inneren Burghof gruppieren sich die Burgschänke, der Saalbau mit dem Festsaal, der Fürstenbau, die Schlosskirche und der Hungerturm (13. Jh.), der als Bergfried diente und zugleich ältester Teil der Burg ist. Ein **Rundgang** durch die Gebäude führt u.a. zu den wertvollen Grabdenkmälern der Grafen von Oettingen und dauert eine knappe Stunde. Vom Burgberg hat der Besucher einen schönen Ausblick über die Harburger Altstadt mit dem gewundenen Flusslauf der Wörnitz, dem Grenzfluss

Harburg

The small medieval town of Harburg is squeezed onto the steep slope between the River Wörnitz and the Burgberg, the hill on which the massive fortress stands. When it was first mentioned in records in 1150 it was still in the possession of the Staufer emperors, having been built to secure the trading route from Augsburg to Nuremberg. 100 years later it was pledged to, and then taken over by, the Counts of Oettingen, together with the town, and it is today in the hands of the charitable ruler of Öttingen.

Never once conquered during the whole of its long history, it is now one of the best preserved castles in Germany. Because of the cramped space, the Romantic Road in the vicinity of the **castle** has to be led through a tunnel 300 metres long. Just before the tunnel, a road climbs up to the right to a car-park below the castle, entrance to which is covered by high walls with a walkway and arrow-slits, and a double gate-tower. The wooden portcullis with its iron tips is still preserved in the inner gate-tower. Around the inner castle courtyard are the Burgschenke or tavern, the Saalbau with a banqueting hall, the Fürstenbau in which the princes lived, the castle chapel, and the Hungerturm (13th century) which served as the castle keep and is at the same time the oldest part of the castle.

A **tour** through the buildings leads to the priceless tombs of the Counts of Oettingen, and lasts a good half-hour.

zwischen der Schwäbischen und der Fränkischen Alb. Durch enge Straßen gelangt der Autofahrer hinunter zur Wörnitz, wo er besonders im Bereich der **alten steinernen Brücke** (1712) mit ihren 7 Bogen einmalige Motive mit dem Fluss, alten Häusern und der Burg entdecken kann. Die Altstadt jedoch sollte er zu Fuß erkunden und sich in aller Ruhe an den schönen Fachwerkhäusern z.B. des ehemaligen Pfarrhauses und des Rathauses erfreuen. Harburgs Wappen, ein schwarzer Adler mit roten Krallen, weist auf den Ursprung der Stadt als Reichsgut hin.

From the castle hill the visitor has a fine view across the old town centre of Harburg and the meandering course of the Wörnitz.

The car-driver can now travel down through narrow streets to the Wörnitz, where he can discover unique views particularly in the vicinity of the **old stone-arched bridge** (1712) with its seven arches, and the old houses huddling below the castle. Harburg's coat-of-arms consist of a black eagle with red weapons, indicating the town's origins as the Emperor's property.

Harburg: historische Gebäude und Wehrgang
Historical buildings with the parapet walk

Repräsentativer Festsaal

Blick auf den oberen Burghof
View to the upper Burghof

Representive celebration room

Donauwörth

An der Mündung der Wörnitz in die Donau liegt Donauwörth (20.000 Einwohner), entstanden aus einer Fischersiedlung auf der Wörnitzinsel (Wörth). Mit dem Bau der ersten Donaubrücke um 975 für die Fernhandelsstraße Augsburg-Nürnberg erlangte „Werd", später „Schwäbischwerd", an Bedeutung und erhielt 1193 das Stadtrecht.

Rückgrat der historischen Altstadt ist die **Reichsstraße** zwischen dem **Rathaus** und dem **Fuggerhaus**. Sie imponiert durch die Geschlossenheit ihrer Häuserzeilen und ist einer der schönsten Straßenzüge Süddeutschlands. Und dies wieder, obwohl die Stadt 1945 zu 75% zerstört worden war. Wegen ihrer enormen Breite hieß sie früher Oberer und Unterer Markt und war im Mittelalter Teil der Handelsstraße. Das Rathaus besteht seit 1236 ununterbrochen, wurde jedoch des Öfteren erweitert und verändert. Über dem Hauptportal mit der harmonischen Doppeltreppe ist das Wappen in der Form angebracht, wie es Karl V. im Jahre 1530 der Stadt verliehen hatte. An der Kapellstraße liegen das **Bürgerspital** mit seiner Kirche (17. Jh.) und das ehemalige **Deutschordenshaus**, dessen klassizistischer

Die Türme des Liebfrauenmünsters und der Heiliggeistkirche in Abendbeleuchtung

Donauwörth

Donauwörth, a town of 20,000 inhabitants, stands at the confluence of the Wörnitz and the Danube. It originated as a fishing village on an island in the Wörnitz called Wörth, and when the first bridge was built across the Danube to carry the Augsburg-Nuremberg trading route the village of „Werd", later „Schwäbischwörth", gained in importance and was granted charter rights in 1193. The backbone of the historical old town centre is the **Reichsstrasse**, running from the **town hall** to the **Fuggerhaus**. It is an imposing street, the buildings along it forming a complete entity, and one of the most beautiful in the whole of southern Germany. Because of its great width it used to be called Oberer Markt and Unterer Markt, and was formed part of the main market street in the Middle Ages. The town hall has stood without interruption since 1236, although it has often been enlarged and altered. Above the main entrance doorway with its harmonious double stairway is the coat-ofarms as granted to the town by Karl V. in 1530. Along the Kapellgasse stand the **Bürgerspital** with its church (17th century) and the former **house of the Deutscher Orden** order of chivalry, a classical-style building con-

The towers of the Liebfrauenmünster and the Holy Ghost church in evening impression

Spätgotisches Liebfrauenmünster

Late gothic Liebfrauenmünster

Historische Giebelhäuser in der Reichsstraße

Historical gable house in the Reichsstreet

Bau einen spätbarocken Festsaal – benannt nach dem berühmten Donauwörther Maler Enderle (1725-1798) – bewahrt. Außerdem ist dort die städtische **Kunstgalerie** eingerichtet. Beim Blick zurück über den Rathausplatz gewahren wir ein hohes Fachwerkhaus, dessen Obergeschosse weit vorkragen. Es gehört zur Spitalgasse, an deren Ende das **Rieder Tor** über eine Brücke uns auf die Insel „Ried" geleitet, den Ursprung der Siedlung. Sowohl das Torgebäude als auch das Hintermeierhaus (ehem. Fischerhaus, 15. Jh.) auf dem „Wörth" enthalten geschichtliche Sammlungen. Das reichsstädtische **Tanzhaus** (15. Jh.) enthielt Verkaufsläden für Bäcker und Fleischer und diente als Schranne. Das Obergeschoss nutzte die Stadt an Markttagen für die Stände von Kaufleuten, bei festlichen Gelegenheiten als Tanzsaal. Seit dem Wiederaufbau von 1975 ist es als Stadtsaal das gesellschaftliche Zentrum.

Schräg gegenüber erhebt sich der spätgotische Backsteinbau des **Liebfrauenmünsters** (1444-67). In seinem massigen Turm hängt seit 1512 Schwabens größte Turmglocke, die 131 Zentner schwere „Pummerin". Schon wegen der herrlichen Aussicht lohnt der Aufstieg zum

taining a late-baroque banqueting hall. Glancing back towards the Rathausplatz we see a tall, half-timbered building, the upper floors of which project a long way forward. It stands in the Spitalgasse, at the far end of which the **Riedertor** leads us out across a bridge to the island called „Ried", which was the original settlement. Both this gateway and the Hintermeierhaus (formerly Fischerhaus, 15th century) on the island of Wörth contain historic collections. The Imperial **Tanzhaus** (15th century), was used as bakers' and fish shops and at the rear as a market hall. The town used the upper floor on market days for merchants' stands, and on high days and holidays as a dance floor.

Diagonally opposite is the late-Gothic brick **Minster** (1444-1467). The biggest church bell in the whole of Swabia has hung in its belfry since 1512; it weighs $6\frac{1}{2}$ tons and is called „Pummerin". It is worth climbing to the top of the church tower just for the magnificent view, and inside the church the soaring sacrament house and the late-Gothic frescoes are also worth a visit. The Renaissance building at the end of the Reichsstrasse is nowadays the Landratsamt or County Council head-

Turmumgang. In der feinsinnig renovierten Hallenkirche sind nicht nur das hoch aufsteigende Sakramentshäuschen und spätgotische Fresken einen Besuch wert.

Das **Fuggerhaus**, den imposanten Renaissancebau am Ende der Reichsstraße, ließ Anton Fugger 1537-39 errichten. Während des 30-jährigen Krieges diente es 1632 Gustav Adolf von Schweden nebst Gemahlin als Quartier, später auch dem „Winterkönig" und Kaiser Karl VI. (1711).

Ein besonders malerisches Reststück der mittelalterlichen Wehrmauer sind der runde Wasserturm und die „Invalidenkaserne" (18. Jh.). Das harmonische Bauwerk

quarters, but it was built t in 1537-39 by Anton Fugger and was used in 1632, during the Thirty Years War, as headquarters by Gustav Adolf of Sweden and his consort, and later by the „Winter King" and by the Emperor Karl VI (1711).

We reach a particularly picturesque remnant of the medieval defensive wall with the round water-tower and the Invalidenkaserne or „infirmary barracks" (18th century) .The late-baroque Heilig-Kreuz-Kirche, the **church of the Holy Cross**,a harmonious structure was built in 1717-22. The tasteful and discreet stucco decorations framing the ceiling frescoes are likewise the products

Donauwörth: Blick über die Donau zur Altstadt

Donauwörth: View over the Donau to the old city

der spätbarocken Heilig-Kreuz-Kirche entstand 1717-22 unter dem berühmten Architekten Joseph Schmuzer aus Wessobrunn.

Alljährlich im Juli spielen beim „Schwäbischwerder Kindertag" 1000 Schülerinnen und Schüler die Geschichte ihrer Stadt, die weithin Reichsgeschichte war. Und im Oktober laden die „Donauwörther Kulturtage" zu Veranstaltungen mit besonderem Niveau.

of Wessobrunn master-craftsmen, and so is the High Altar, which came from the brother of the architect of the church. Jearly in July on the Schwäbischwerder Kindertag 1000 Children play the history of the city. In October the Danauwörther Kulturtage (culture days) invite to events of special high standard quality.

Käthe-Kruse's Puppen ->

Käthe-Kruse's dolls ->

Vor der Kulisse des Rieder Tors   *Backtrop of the Rieder Tor*

Reichsstraßenfest   *Reichsstreet festival*   **Wörnitz mit Rieder Tor**   *Wörtnitz with Rieder tower*

Rain am Lech

Etwa 15 km östlich von Donauwörth liegt das Städtchen Rain (8500 Ew.). Im Jahr 1260 wurde es bereits als „herzogliche Stadt" erwähnt, die als nordwestliche Grenzbefestigung Altbayerns von Bedeutung war. Sie erlangte deshalb Stadt-, Markt- und Zollrechte. Noch heute zeugen Reste der Stadtbefestigung sowie das Schwabtor, ehemals befestigte Einfahrt aus Richtung Norden, von der Wehrhaftigkeit der einstigen Festung. Sehenswert ist die Ansammlung von historischen Bürgerhäusern des 17. und 18. Jahrhunderts in der Hauptstraße. Im deren Zentrum imponiert das kunstvoll gestaltete Rokoko-Rathaus. Das Tilly-Denkmal auf dem Rathausplatz erinnert an den berühmten kaiserlichen Feldherrn des 30-jährigen Krieges und seine schicksalhafte Verbindung mit Rain: Nahe der Stadt stellte er sich

Rain am Lech

About 15 km to the east is the little city of Rain, about (8500 inhabitants). In 1260 it was mentioned as the „Dukes City" which was the northwest border to old Bavaria. Even today rests of the town wall and the Schwabtor, former affixed gateway from the north shows what a great defence forttress it was. Worth seeing is the conglomeration of historical buildings of the 17th and 18th Century on the main street. In the centre impresses the artisticly built rococo town hall. The Tilly memorial on the market square reminds of the famous imperial commander of the 30 year war. Near the city in 1632 he lead the Bavarian heer against the swedish king Gustav Adolf to the battle near Rain. He was injured hard on his leg and had to give up and returned to Ingoldstadt where he deceased only 2 weeks later.

Rathaus mit Tilly-Denkmal   *City hall with Tilly monument*

**Dehner Blumenpark
& Naturlehrgarten**

*Dehner flowerpark
with natural garden*

1632 mit dem bayerischen Heer dem Schwedenkönig Gustav Adolf zur „Schlacht bei Rain". Er wurde schwer am Bein verwundet und musste sich geschlagen nach Ingolstadt zurückziehen, wo er zwei Wochen später als Folge der Verletzung starb.

Die katholische Stadtpfarrkirche St. Johannes der Täufer (um 1480) besitzt wertvolle spätgotische Fresken und ist daher ebenso einen Besuch wert wie das Spital mit der Allerheiligenkapelle, das Geburtshaus der Musiker-Brüder Lachner, das man in ein Museum umwandelte und der großzügige „Dehner Blumen Park", den die Gartencenter-Kette am Ort ihres Stammsitzes anlegen ließ. Das bekannteste Großereignis ist das Stadtfest, das alljährlich am zweiten Juliwochenende die Massen anzieht.

The catholic church of St. John the Baptist, was built in about 1480 owns precious late gothic frescoes and is therefore worth a visit like the Spital with Allerhei-ligenkapelle, the birth place of the musician brothers Lochner which has been turned into a museum and the bountiful flower park „Dehner" which has been created in their ancestral seat. An accumulation of flowers, and plants is a pleasure for the eyes and mind recreation. The most famous event is the city festival which is yearly on the second weekend in July. The wide low land invites to bycicle tors in the region.

Only a few kilometers eastward is the renaissance city Neuburg/ Donau. On the south of it Donaumoos, southern Germany's biggest marsh of which near Pöttmes quite an area is still maintained.

Augsburg

Die Stadt entwickelte sich im Laufe von über 2000 Jahren aus einem römischen Heerlager unter Kaiser Augustus (15. v. Chr.), der im Namen der Stadt fortlebt. Durch ihre bevorzugte Lage am Schnittpunkt wichtiger Handelsstraßen erlangte sie im Mittelalter große Bedeutung, die im Zeitalter der reichen Fugger (um 1500) und der Seefahrerdynastie der Welser Augsburg zur Weltstadt werden ließ. Kaiserbesuche und Reichstage wurden zur Gewohnheit, berühmte Künstler arbeiteten in der Stadt, die in der Renaissance zum Zentrum von Architektur, Musik und Malerei avancierte. Heute ist Augsburg die drittgrößte Stadt Bayerns, gleichzeitig Sitz einer Universität und der Regierung von Schwaben sowie ein bedeutender Wirtschaftsstandort. Das Stadtwappen mit einem grünen Pinienzapfen erinnert an ihre römische Vergangenheit, als Augsburg römische Provinzhauptstadt war, der Augsburger Religionsfrieden an den bisher längsten Frieden der deutschen Geschichte.

Augsburg

The town has developed over a period of 2000 years, starting as a Roman military camp under the Emperor Augustus (15 BC), whose name lives on in that of the city. Because of its advantageous position at the crossroads of major trading routes, it achieved considerable importance in the Middle Ages and world fame during the time of the wealthy Fugger family (around 1500) and the sea-faring dynasty of Weiser. Visits by the Emperor and sessions of the Reichstag or Imperial Parliament became everyday events, famous artists worked in the city, and it advanced during the Renaissance to become a centre of architecture, music, and painting. Today it is the third largest city in Bavaria and also a university city and the centre of the government district of Swabia, quite apart from also being a major commercial centre. On the city's 1600th jubilee in 1594, the city had the **Augustus fountain** erected in front of the town hall to the honour of its founder. The four figures around the

Maximilian-Straße
Maximilian-Street

Der Augustusbrunnen zu Ehren des römischen Stadtgründers

Anlässlich ihres 1600-jährigen Jubiläums ließ die Stadt zu Ehren ihres römischen Gründers 1594 den **Augustusbrunnen** vor dem Rathaus errichten. Die vier Beckenfiguren symbolisieren die Flüsse, deren Wasserkraft seit alten Zeiten wichtige Hilfe für viele Handwerksbetriebe in Augsburg war. Das **Rathaus** errichtete der bedeutendste Baumeister, Elias Holl, zwischen 1615 und 1620. Es ist einer der schönsten und wichtigsten Profanbauten der Renaissance nördlich der Alpen. Einmalig in seiner prunkvollen Ausstattung ist der Goldene Saal mit herrlichen Portalen, Wandmalereien und einer kunstvollen Kassettendecke. Neben dem Rathaus bildet der nahe **Perlachturm** das zweite Wahrzeichen Augsburgs. Über dem mittelalterlichen Kern des ehemaligen Wehrturms entstanden, wiederum unter Elias Holl, die Obergeschosse mit der Glockenlaterne und der für Augsburg typischen „Welschen Haube" als Abschluss. Vom Umgang des 70 m hohen Turms hat man eine herrliche Aussicht über den Stadtkern. Die Pfeile der grünen Hinweistafeln führen uns zur **Kirche „Maria Stern"** , einst Gotteshaus des Franziskanerinnenklosters. Erbaut 1574-76 unter Johannes Holl, dem Vater des Rathauserbauers, entstand hier erstmals als Turmabschluss die genannte „Welsche

The Augustus fountain in honour of the roman city founder

basin symbolise the four rivers which have from the earliest days provided the vital water power for Augsburg craft enterprises. The **Rathaus** was built by the most famous of all local architects, Elias Holl, between 1615 and 1620. It is one of the most beautiful and significant buildings of the Renaissance, other than churches, anywhere north of the Alps. The Goldener Saal is unique with its magnificent doorways, wallpaintings, and an artistic cassetted ceiling. Augsburg's second landmark after the Rathaus is the nearby **Perlachturm**; towering over the medieval core of the former defensive tower, and likewise designed by Elias Holl, the upper storeys carry the lantern belfry and are topped by the Welsche Haube, a typical feature of Augsburg. From the top of the 70-metre tall tower there is a magnificent view over the old town centre. The arrows on the green signposts lead us to a **church, Maria Stern**, once the chapel of the Franciscan monastery. Built in 1574-76 under the direction of Johannes Holl, the father of the builder of the Rathaus, this was the first tower to be capped with a Welsche Haube, which is also known as an „Augsburg onion". One of the most striking buildings in the city is the **Fuggerei**, the oldest alms houses anywhere in the

Rathaus und Perlachturm sind die Wahrzeichen der Stadt

City hall and the Perlach tower: the town's landmark

Haube", auch „Augsburger Zwiebel" genannt. Mit der **Fuggerei** haben wir eine der markantesten Anlagen der Stadt und die älteste Sozialsiedlung der Welt überhaupt vor uns. Gegründet 1516 durch Jakob Fugger den Reichen und seine Brüder, umfasst sie 67 Häuschen mit 140 Kleinwohnungen, eine Kirche, einen Brunnen und eine Ummauerung mit Toren, bildet also eine Stadt in der Stadt. Gemäß den damaligen Bedingungen müssen die

world, so called because they were built by the wealthy Fugger family. They were endowed in 1516 by Jakob Fugger the Wealthy and his brothers, and consist of 67 cottages containing 147 small apartments, a church, a fountain, and a surrounding wall with gateways, in effect a town within a town. According to the stipulations made at the time, the inhabitants must even today be poor, of blameless behaviour, citizens of Augsburg, and

Der goldene Saal im Rathaus

The golden room in the town hall

Bewohner auch heute arm, unbescholten, Augsburger Bürger und katholisch sein, jährlich 0,88 € (Gegenwert eines rheinischen Guldens) Miete bezahlen und laut Hausordnung täglich drei Gebete für die Stifter beten. Der **Ulrichsstadel** war Stall- und Stadelbau des einst reichsunmittelbaren Benediktinerstifts **St. Ulrich und Afra**. Die spätgotische Basilika besitzt eine wertvolle

Catholic. They pay an annual rent of 0,88 €, the equivalent of one Rhinish Guilder, and have to say a prayer three times a day for the founder. The most southerly, and also the strongest, of the defensive bulwarks was the Rote-Tor-Bastei, where nowadays a **herb garden** and an **open-air theatre** take the place of the former moat – now, happily, no longer required. The **Rotes Tor**

**Die „Fuggerei"
entstand ab 1516**

*The „Fuggerei"
developed from 1516*

**Der Herkulesbrunnen
vor der Basilika
St. Ulrich und Afra**

*The Hercules
Fountain in front
of the basilica
St. Ulrich and Afra*

Schaezler-Palais, Deutsche Barock- und Staatsgalerie

Schaezler-Palais, German Baroque Galery and State Galery

Ausstattung sowohl im Renaissance- als im Barock-stil, ebenso im ehemaligen Predigersaal, der heutigen evangelischen Ulrichskirche. In der Maximilianstraße steht mit dem **Schaezler-Palais** der beeindruckendste Bau des Rokoko in Augsburg. Neben dem 23 m langen, prächtigen Festsaal mit Schnitz- und Stuckdekorationen, Wandspiegeln und Deckenfresken sind heute auch die Deutsche Barockgalerie und die Staatsgalerie dort untergebracht.

Der nahe **Herkulesbrunnen** entstand um 1600, ebenso wie der **Merkurbrunnen**. Beide sind Arbeiten des Niederländers Adrian de Vries. Dazwischen gefallen die **Fuggerhäuser**, entstanden 1512-15 als Wohn- und Geschäftshaus von Jakob Fugger mit reizvollen Innenhöfen (Damenhof), das **Zeughaus** von 1607 (E. Holl. Prunkfassade) sowie das ehemalige **Chorherrenstift St. Moritz** mit Resten seiner Barockausstattung. Die ehemalige Karmeliter-Klosterkirche (1321, erweitert 15. Jh., der hl. Anna geweiht), enthält gotische Wandmalereien und wertvolle Gemälde, u. a. von Lucas Cranach dem Älteren sowie die Grabkapelle der Fugger von

dates from 1622, redesigned by Elias Holl, nowadays forms part of a romantic park. The late-Gothic basilica possesses a valuable interior, in both the Renaissance and the baroque style, and a former sermon hall which today is the Evangelical church of St Ulrich. On the lefthand side stands one of Augsburg's most impressive rococo palaces, the **Schaezler-Palais**. Apart from its magnificent banqueting hall, 23 metres long and rich in carvings and stucco decorations, wall mirrors and ceiling frescoes, it is nowadays also the home of the German Baroque Gallery and the State Gallery.

The nearby **Herkulesbrunnen** was created in about 1600, also, the **Merkurbrunnen**. Both are the work of the Dutch artist Adrian de Vries, we should look at the **Fuggerhäuser**, built in 1512-15 as residential homes and business premises by Jakob Fugger, with their charming internal courtyards. **St Anna's church** , a former Carmelite monastery church (1321, enlarged in the 15th century) contains Gothic wall decorations and valuable paintings, including some by Lucas Cranach the Elder, and the sepulchre chapel of the Fuggers

Schaezler-Palais, Rokokosaal

Schaezler Palais, Rokokosaal

1518, den ältesten sakralen Renaissancebau nördlich der Alpen. Im letztgenannten Jahr wohnte Martin Luther während seiner Verhandlungen mit dem päpstlichen Legaten Cajetan im angrenzenden Klosterbau, wo heute eine Gedenkstätte (Lutherstiege) zu besichtigen ist. Die Kirche wird seit 1525 evangelisch genutzt . Während das **Peutingerhaus** (16. Jh., feine Rokokofassade von 1763) und der bischöfliche **Hofgarten** etwas abseits im südlichen Bereich des Domes liegen, grenzt die ehemalige **Residenz** an den Dom. Lediglich der Turm blieb vom mittelalterlichen Fronhof erhalten. Die übrigen Gebäude entstanden im 18. Jahrhundert und werden heute von der Regierung von Schwaben als Residenz genutzt. Am 25.6.1530 wurde im damaligen Kapitelsaal die „Augsburgische Konfession" verkündet, das grundlegende Bekenntnis der lutherischen Kirche. Der **Dom**, wurde bereits 823 in Urkunden genannt. Fast so alt sind die Krypta (10. Jh.) und die Glasmalereien (12. Jh.), die zu den ältesten in Deutschland zählen. Decken- und Wandfresken aus romanischer und gotischer Zeit sowie Tafelbilder von Hans Holbein d. Ä. lassen den Dom zu einem Augenschmaus für Liebhaber sakraler Kunst werden.

Augsburger Dom   *Augsburg Cathedral*

Mozartkonzert im Rokokosaal
Mozart concert in the Rokokohall

Augsburger Puppenkiste   *Augsburger Doll Cabinet*

which they used from 1509 to 1518. As the church was used for Evangelical services from 1525 onwards, the Fuggers gave up their sepulchre chapel. Whilst the **Peutingerhaus** a fine rococo façade dating from 1763) and the **garden of the bishops' palace** lie a little off to one side of our main route, we will concentrate on the **Residenz** am Fronhof, near the cathedral. The tower is all that has been preserved from the medieval Fronhof; the remaining buildings date from the 18th century, and are now used as a residence by the government of Swabia. On 25th June 1530 the „Augsburg Confession" was promulgated in the Chapter Room, which was then still in existence; this is the basic confession of the Lutheran church. Only a few metres separate the bishops' palace from their own church, the **cathedral**, which was first mentioned in historical records as long ago as 823. Ceiling and wall frescoes from the Roman and Gothic periods, panel paintings by Hans Holbein Senior, and a bronze door (about 1356, with 35 bas-relief illustrations) make the cathedral a treat for the eyes of any lover of church art.

Perlach-Turm und Renaissance-Rathaus
The Perlach Tower and Renaissance Town hall

Friedberg

Entstanden war die einstige Festungsstadt um 1264 als herzogliche Grenzbefestigung der Wittelsbacher vor allem gegen die drei Augsburger Territorien der Freien Reichsstadt, des Bistums und des reichsfreien Benediktinerklosters St. Ulrich und Afra sowie gegen Schwaben. Schon von Weitem grüßen wehrhafte Festungsmauern, Bastionen und Türme auf uns herab. Die heutige noch teilweise erhaltene Befestigung entstand anfangs des 15. Jahrhunderts, wie eine spätgotische Gedenktafel in der Westwand der St.-Jakobs-Kirche (19. Jh.) verkündet. Neben den Resten der Stadtmauer – vor allem in der Südwestecke der Anlage – gefällt vor allem der zentral gelegene **Marienplatz** mit dem hübschen Brunnen, der Mariensäule, und dem schmucken Rathaus, das die Friedberger 1674 im Stil des Augsburgers Elias Holl errichteten. Das **Schloss** über **Friedberg** entstand 1552-59 auf dem Platz einer älteren Anlage (13. Jh.) der Wittelsbacher. Heute ist dort ein Museum untergebracht. Es zeigt u.a. eine bemerkenswerte Sammlung der hier für kurze Zeit arbeitenden Fayencen-Manufaktur und der früher berühmten Friedberger Uhren sowie eine umfangreiche Auswahl der Friedberger Handwerkskunst. Östlich vom Stadtkern liegt die **Wallfahrtskirche** Herrgottsruh, die ihren Namen nach dem Gnadenbild (um 1496) trägt. Es zeigt den erschöpften Christus, der sich vom Tragen des Kreuzes ausruht. Das Gotteshaus entstand 1731-53 und gefällt besonders durch seine schwerelos wirkenden Gewölbe mit ausgezeichneten Kuppelfresken und kunstvollen Stuckaturen des Wessobrunner Meisters Feichtmayr.

Marienplatz mit Rathaus und Brunnen

Marienplatz with town hall and fountain

Das Schloss über Friedberg (1552-1559)

The castle above Friedberg (1552-1559)

**Stadtbefestigung ->
15. Jahrhundert**

*Town Wall of the ->
15th century*

Friedberg

Friedberg was created in 1264 as the frontier fortifications of the Dukes of Wittelsbach mainly against the three Augsburg territories of the Free Imperial City, the See, and the Imperial Benedictine monastery of St Ulrich and St Afra, but also against the Swabians generally. The sturdy defensive walls, bastions, and towers look down on us and welcome us from a long way away. The defences are still partly preserved today; they were built at the beginning of the 15th century, as a late-Gothic plaque in the west wall of St Jacob's church (19th century) commemorates. Apart from the remains of the town wall, principally the part in the south-west corner, the most pleasing feature is the central **Marienplatz** with its pretty fountain, the Mariensäule column, and the neat town hall, built by the citizens of Friedberg in 1674 in the style of Augsburg's Elias Holl. The **palace** up above Friedberg was built in 1552-59 on the site of a 13th century Wittelsbach castle, and today houses a museum of local arts and crafts. Among other things, it offers a remarkable collection illustrating the faience manufacture, the once famous Friedberg clocks and a wide selection of Friedberg handiwork.

East of the centre of the town lies the **pilgrimage church** of Hergottsruh, which takes its name („The Peace of God") from the famous Picture of Grace (about 1496), which shows an Jesus resting, exhausted from carrying the Cross. This church was built in 1731-35, and its particularly pleasing feature is its vaulted ceiling, with its outstanding cupola frescoes and artistic stucco work from the Wessobrunn master Feichtmayr.

Wehrturm im Abendlicht

Defence tower in the sunset light

Unten rechts: Wallfahrtskirche Herrgottsruh, Gnadenbild

Down right: The pilgrimage church of Herrgottsruh, the Picture of Grace

Landsberg
am Lech

Dank seiner günstigen Lage steil über einem Lechübergang ist der Schlossberg immer wieder besiedelt worden. Ausgrabungen wiesen bronzezeitliche (um 1800-1200 v. Chr.) und urnenfelderzeitliche Besiedlung (um 1250-750 v. Chr.) ebenso nach wie eine spätrömische (300-400 n. Chr.).Heinrich der Löwe ließ dann 1160 eine „Landespurch" zur Sicherung der Salzstraße errichten, die von Reichenhall zum Bodenseegebiet führte. Die zu entrichtende Salzsteuer trug maßgeblich zum Reichtum der Stadt im Mittelalter bei. Noch heute liegt Landsberg sehr zentral und verkehrsmäßig bestens erschlossen durch die Nord-Süd-Verbindung der B 17 und die quer verlaufende Autobahn A 96 München – Lindau.

Landsberg
am Lech

The Schlossberg, a steep hill above the crossing-point of the River Lech, has often been the site of a settlement on account of its favourable position. Excavations indicate a bronze-age settlement (about 1800-1200 BC) and a potteryage settlement (about 1250-750 BC), as well as one in the later Roman era (300-400 AD). Henry the Lion then had a castle, the „Landespurch", built to secure the Salt Road, which led from Reichenhall to Lake Constance. The „salt tax" which had to be paid contributed substantially to the wealth of the town in the Middle Ages.

Even today, Landsberg has a very central location and can be easily reached by all means of transport, in par-

Gesamtansicht mit Stadtmuseum, Heiligkreuzkirche und Bayertor

General view with the city museum, holy cross church and Bavarian gate

Marienbrunnen, dahinter das barocke Rathaus

The market fountain behind the baroque town hall

Der 30 Meter hohe Mutterturm, erbaut 1884-1888

The 30-metre tall Mutterturm was built in 1884-1888

Mitten auf dem weiten Hauptplatz im Zentrum stand einst das alte Rathaus. Der heutige Bau (um 1700) ist in die westliche Häuserzeile integriert, sticht aber durch seine reich verzierte Stuckfassade deutlich heraus. Sie ist ein Werk des Architekten der berühmten Wieskirche, Dominikus Zimmermann, der auch die Räume im Obergeschoss stuckierte. Unter seiner Leitung war um 1752 die Johanniskirche in Landsberg entstanden, von 1749-54 war er hier Bürgermeister, fast zeitgleich mit dem von ihm geleiteten Bau der Wieskirche (1746-54), seinem Lebenswerk. Vor dem Rathaus steht ein schöner **Marktbrunnen** (1783) mit Marienfigur.

Am Lech lohnt ein kurzer Abstecher über die Brücke und entlang der Promenade rechts wegen der schönen Stadtansicht. Ein kurioses Turmhaus am westlichen Ufer, der „**Mutterturm**", entstand Ende des 19. Jahrhunderts als Wohnhaus und Atelier des Malers und Graphikers von Herkomer, dessen Kunstsammlung noch heute hier ausgestellt ist.

ticular thanks to the road B 17 – from the north to the south – and to the motorway A96 Munich-Lindau – from the east to the west. The Rathaus, (about 1700) a richly decorated stucco façade is a piece of work from Dominikus Zimmermann, the same architect as the one who created the famous Wieskirche, who also did the stucco work in the upper storey. It was under his direction that St John's church in Landsberg was built in 1752, and he was mayor from 1749 to 1754, almost exactly the period of time when he was supervising the building of his life's work, the famous Wieskirche (1746-54). A beautiful **fountain** (1783) stands in front of the town hall with a statue of the Virgin Mary.

The River Lech is worth making a short diversion across the bridge and along the promenade to the right, to gain a fine view of the city. One curious tower building stands on the west bank – the **Mutterturm**, built at the end of the 19th century as the residence and studio of the painter and draftsman Hubert von Herkomer. A

Blick über das Wehr auf das östliche Lechufer

View across the damm on the east bank of the Lech

Während das äußere **Färbertor** um 1560 mit der Stadt-erweiterung entstand, steht das **Bäckertor** hinter dem Lechkanal bereits seit dem 15. Jahrhundert. Die **Johanniskirche** passt sich dem harmonisch gewachsenen Straßenbild mit dem abschließenden **Sandauer Tor** (um 1630) gut an. An diesen nördlichen Torturm grenzt der **Staffingerhof** an, einst Sitz des 1556 gegründeten Landsberger Bundes. Er existierte bis 1599 und hatte sich die Abwehr des Protestantismus zum Ziel gesetzt. Danach gelangte das Gebäude samt dem schönen Arkadenhof, auch als Turnierhof genutzt, in den Besitz der Herzöge von Bayern. Am Hinteren Anger erhebt sich die mächtige **Stadtpfarrkirche** Mariä Himmelfahrt (15. Jh.). Sie besitzt herrliche Glasgemälde (16. Jh.) und Stuckarbeiten sowie Schnitzarbeiten von Lorenz Luidl (Palmesel) und Hans Multscher (Multscher Madonna).

collection of his work can still be seen exhibited here. The outer **Fäbertor** was built in about 1560, when the town was being expanded, the **Bäckertor** has been standing here behind the canalised section of the River Lech since the 15th century. The **church of St John**, mentioned before, fits perfectly into the overall view of the town, which has grown harmoniously over the centuries, and with the **Sandauer Tor** (about 1630). Immediately adjacent to this north gate of the town is the **Staffingerhof**, once the home of the Landsberger Bund, an organisation founded in 1556 and which existed until 1599 with the aim of defending the town from Protestantism. The building with its lovely Arkadenhof, passed into the possession of the Dukes of Bavaria and was used as a riding school. Along the Hinterer Anger, we see the massive **parish church** of St Mary of the

Treppen helfen uns beim Überwinden des Höhenunterschieds hinauf zum Gelände des ehemaligen **Jesuitenklosters**. Neben dem Portal der Heilig-Kreuz-Kirche (1752-54) befindet sich der Eingang zum schönen Arkadenhof, der zum Jesuitenkolleg gehörte. Die von außen schmucklose Kirche besticht durch die Pracht des Barock und Rokoko im Innenraum, mit Stuckornamenten und Fresken, Gemälden und feinen Schnitzarbeiten an den Beichtstühlen. Im ehemaligen Jesuitengymnasium hat die Stadt ihr neues **Museum** eingerichtet. Neben zahlreichen Zeugnissen des bürgerlichen Lebens sind es vor allem Kunstwerke aus den zahlreichen Gotteshäusern, von denen Landsberg zur Zeit des Rokoko bei 2000 Einwohnern immerhin 11 besaß. Eine der wertvollsten Plastiken ist die spätgotische Darstellung der Krönung Mariens. Beim imposanten **Bayertor** ermöglicht der 36 m hohe Turm einen ungehinderten Ausblick über die Altstadt und – bei guter Sicht – bis hin zu den Ketten der Alpen. Das malerisch verwinkelte Hexenviertel ziert der schöne Turm. Da in seiner Durchfahrt früher die Bauern ihre Erzeugnisse verkauften, heißt er im Volksmund auch **Schmalzturm**. Der repräsentative Wehrbau entstand im 13. Jh. und gehörte zur ältesten Stadtbefestigung.

Ascension (15th century). It possesses some magnificent glass windows (16th century) and stucco work, as well as carvings by Lorenz Luidl (the Palm Sunday donkey and the Madonna of Hans Multscher).

The former **Jesuit monastery**. Next to the doorway of the Heilig- Kreuz-Kirche (1752-54) is the entrance to the beautiful Arkadenhof, which belonged to the Jesuit college. The church, plain and undecorated on the outside, overwhelms the visitor with the magnificence of the baroque and rococo interior, with ornamental stucco and frescoes, paintings, and the fine wood carvings of the confessional boxes. The city has arranged its **museum** in the former Jesuit school. One of the most valuable pieces is a late Gothic sculpture depicting the coronation of the Virgin Mary.

The rectangular **Bayertor**, a 36-metre tall tower provides a view over the town and, if the weather permits, across to the ranks of the Alps. From the Schlossberg we can enjoy the view before diving down through the picturesque, higgledypiggledy Hexenviertel to the **Schöner Turm** or „beautiful tower". Because farmers passing through it sold such produce as goose-dripping, it is also known popularly as the **Schmalzturm**. This imposing defensive tower was built in the 13th century and was part of the oldest sections of the town defences.

Das repräsentative Bayertor (15. Jh.) ist einer der größten gotischen Wehrbauten einer Stadtbefestigung in ganz Bayern

The imposing Bayertor (15th century) is one of the largest Gothic defensive towers belonging to town fortifications anywhere in Bavaria

Hohenfurch

Die Romantische Straße durchschneidet das Dorf Hohenfurch, das in oberbayerisch-ländlicher Umgebung zu einem geruhsamen Urlaub einlädt. Inmitten einer Vielzahl von herrlichen Kirchen und Klöstern gelegen, bildet es die nördliche Pforte zum Pfaffenwinkel hier im Alpenvorland. Der Ort besitzt eine für dörfliche Verhältnisse sehr schöne **Kirche**, deren Turm und Chor aus dem 14./15. Jahrhundert stammen. Um 1750 wurden der Chor und das spätgotische Langhaus im Stil des Rokoko umgestaltet und zusammen mit den drei Altären 1754 geweiht. Auch die restliche Innenausstattung stammt überwiegend aus dieser Zeit. Durch die hohen Fenster des Langhauses und die zart getönten Wessobrunner Stuckarbeiten wirkt der Innenraum hell und freundlich und lässt die Fresken, Bilder und Schnitzfiguren voll zur Wirkung kommen.

Hohenfurch: prächtige Dorfkirche im Stil des Rokoko (18. Jahrhundert)

Hohenfurch

The Romantic Road slices through the village of Hohenfurch, which invites the traveller to stay for a holiday amidst the surroundings of Upper Bavaria. Set amidst a huge number of magnificent churches and monasteries, it represents the northern gateway to the Pfaffenwinkel, a region in the foothills of the Alps. Hohenfurch has a particularly fine **church** in relation to its village status, with a tower and Choir dating from the 14th or 15th century. The Choir and the late-Gothic nave were rebuilt in about 1750 in the rococo style, and consecrated together with the three altars in 1754. The remainder of the interior likewise dates from about this time. The tall windows of the nave and the delicately shaded Wessobrunn stucco work make the interior bright, and shows off the frescoes, pictures, and carved figures particularly well.

Hohenfurch: gorgeous village church in the rococo style (18th century)

Schongau

Schongau

Wer die Anhöhe von Schongau erreicht, dem öffnet sich der Blick auf das festliche Land zwischen Ammer und Lech, im Süden begrenzt durch die wald- und wasserreichen Vorberge, dahinter die Hochwelt der Alpen. Inmitten dieser uralten Kulturlandschaft, dem „Pfaffenwinkel", liegt, umflossen vom Lech, das Bergstädtchen Schongau.

Reaching the heights of Schongau means being compensated by a wonderful view of the joyful landscape between Ammer and Lech, the Pre-Alps to the south with forests and lakes and, behind, the imposing Alps. In the middle of this ancient cultural region called "Pfaffenwinkel" (= the clerical corner) we can find the mountain village of Schongau, surrounded by the river Lech.

Der Marienplatz, benannt nach der Brunnensäule, dahinter die Stadtkirche Mariä Himmelfahrt

A view across the Marienplatz, named after the tall fountain of St. Mary, with the church in the back

Das Bild der Stadt mit ihren mittelalterlichen Mauern, Toren und Türmen ist ein lebendiger Beweis für ihre reiche Geschichte. Bereits Anfang des 13. Jahrhunderts erhielt sie eigene Rechte, war später Verwaltungsmittelpunkt, Nebenresidenz und Grenzfeste Bayerns. Gegenüber dem heutigen Rathaus von 1926 erhebt sich die barocke Stadtpfarrkirche Mariä Himmelfahrt. Der Neubau auf den Fundamenten eines romanischgotischen Vorgängerbaus wurde 1753 errichtet und von Dominikus Zimmermann, dem Wiesbaumeister, stuckiert. Das Hauptthema der Kirche ist das Leben Mariens, das sich bereits im Hochaltar mit der Auf-

The image of the town with its medieval wall, its gates and towers bears witness of its significant history. At the beginning of the 13th century Schongau was granted municipal rights and later on it was an important administrative centre, a secondary residential palace and Bavaria's border fortress. Opposite the town hall stands the parish church of Our Lady of the Assumption, externally a rather plain building, with a tower and a Choir dating from the 17th century and a nave from 1753. The numerous frescoes and statues inside the church all relate to the life of the Blessed Virgin, and her statue also stands in the centre

Die barocke Stadtpfarrkirche Mariä Himmelfahrt

nahme Mariens in den Himmel zeigt. Einzigartig ist der Volksaltar, der aus der Zeit des ersten Kirchenbaus aus der Romanik erhalten ist. Bemerkenswert sind die Zunftstangen, die kunstvoll gearbeitet die Handwerkszünfte mit ihren Heiligen zeigen.

Südlich der Kirche breitet sich der Marienplatz, nach Süden abgeschlossen durch den Stufengiebel des Ballenhauses. Hinter dem Tor an der Wehrmauer erhebt sich der Polizeidienerturm, mit 17,25 m höchster Wehrbau der Stadt und in früheren Zeiten bewachter Einlass für späte Gäste oder Heimkehrer. Von hier, dem Südende der Altstadt, haben wir einen schönen Blick zum Lech und auf die Berge.

Der folgende Eckturm ist mit 15 m nur unwesentlich kleiner als sein Nachbar. Gegenüber steht die Heiliggeistkirche, die für das 1719 gegründete Karmeliterkloster erbaut wurde. Die an sich zurückhaltende Ausstattung einer typischen Bettelordenskirche wird überstrahlt von den doch recht ansehnlichen sieben Altären, der wertvollen Orgel und vor allem der prächtigen Kanzel, Stiftung eines wohlhabenden Handwerkerehepaars. Der Durchgang am Klostergebäude führt zum Klosterhof mit einem eindrucksvollen Kruzifix. Vom Wehrgang der alten Stadtmauer eröffnen sich reizvolle Blickwinkel

The baroque city church Mariä ascension

of the High Altar, amidst many others. The ceiling paintings in the Choir show the Holy Trinity welcoming the Virgin Mary into heaven.

South of the church is the broad Marienplatz, the southern boundary of which is formed by the stepped gable of the Ballenhaus. On the other side of the gateway ,along the defensive wall is the Polizeidienerturm, which is 17.25 metres tall and thus the tallest fortification in the town. In the old days it was the well-guarded gate that admitted last-minute guests or inhabitants returning home late. From here, the southernmost end of the old town centre, we have a fine view over the Lech and towards the Alps. The next tower, the Eckturm, is 15 metres tall, only slightly smaller than its neighbour. On the left-hand side is the Holy Ghost Church, built in 1719 for the Carmelite monastery. They were actually an Order committed to poverty and begging, and their church as such is correspondingly modest, so that the seven fine altars, the priceless organ, and principally the magnificent pulpit, donated by a wealthy craftsman and his wife, dominate the interior completely. The town wall with its walkway is a charming panorama viewpoint to the north.In addition to three statues on the High Altar produced by mayor Pöllandt (1697), already mentioned, the stagelike Choir

in Richtung Norden. In der St.-Sebastians-Kirche, geweiht 1774 ist neben drei Hochaltar-Figuren des Bürgermeisters Pöllandt (1697) besonders der bühnenartig anmutende Choraltar sehenswert. Auf dem Oberbild des rechten Seitenaltars ist der hl. Magnus mit Drachen dargestellt, der Schutzpatron gegen Garten- und Feldungeziefer: Laut Rechnungen des Stadtkämmerers wurde im 17. und 18. Jahrhundert mehrmals der Stab des Heiligen aus Füssen herbeigeschafft, um der Mäuseplage Herr zu werden. An der breiten Münzstraße blicken wir auf das Münzgebäude, das später als Gefängnis genutzt wurde und heute die Polizei beherbergt.

Hinter dem Königstor (1331) sehen wir bald unterhalb des Hangs die Wallfahrtskirche „Heiligkreuz". Als Nachfolger einer hölzernen Kapelle errichtete Johann Schmuzer 1690-93 den heutigen Hauptbau und auch 1725 eine Erweiterung.

Das Maxtor war einst gleichzeitig Hoftor des Schlosses Schongau. Ein Fresko über dem Torbogen erinnert an die Stadtrechtsverleihung durch Kaiser Ludwig den Bayern 1331. Oberhalb steht Schloss Schongau, im 15. Jahrhundert Kleinresidenz der Wittelsbacher.

altar is also worth mentioning. The upper picture of the right-hand side-altar illustrates St Magnus fighting a dragon; he is the patron saints of gardens and fields, and protects them from pests. According to invoices from 17th and 18th century the pest officers, the Staff of this Saint was fetched several times from Füssen in attempt to master plagues of mice. From the Obere Münzstrasse we turn right and look at the Münzgebäude, originally the „mint" or treasury and later used as a prison; today it is the police station.

Schongau held the privilege of minting its own coins from 1331 to 1750, but the present building was not built until 1771. Passing through the Königstor (1331), we see the Heiligkreuz pilgrimage church at the bottom of the hills. Replacing an early wooden chapel, the main part of the present-day building was built by Joseph Schmuzer in 1690-93, as was an extension in 1725.

The Maxtor used to double the castle gateway to the Schloss Schongau. A fresco above the gateway arch commemorates the granting of municipal rights by Emperor Ludwig the Bavarian in 1331. Above it stands Schloss Schongau, built in the 15th century.

Blick auf die wehrhafte Stadt Schongau aus der Vogelperspektive

From a birds eye view on Schongau

Basilika von Altenstadt   *Basilica of Altenstadt*

Stadtfest   *City festival*

Ostallgäu: Felder, Wiesen, Wälder und Seen, im Hintergrund die Bergketten der Alpen

Eastern Allgäu: fields, woods and sees, in the background the Alps

Peiting

Ähnlich groß wie Schongau ist sein Nachbar, der Markt Peiting. Der Ort taucht 1055 in einer Urkunde auf, als Graf Welf IV. auf dem Schlossberg eine neue Burg errichten ließ. Die Pfarrkirche St. Michael weist Spuren auf aus der großen Vergangenheit des Ortes: Die unteren Teile des Turmes und die Säulen des Altarunterbaus stammen aus der Bauzeit der ersten Steinkirche um 1055, der Taufstein ist 1331 datiert.

Peiting

Markt Peiting is similar in size to its neighbour Schongau and appears in historical records in 1055, when Count Welf IV had a new castle built on the Schlossberg. The **parish church** of St Michael shows any traces of the town's significant past; the lower part of the tower and the columns beneath the altar date from the time when the first stone church was built, in about 1055. The font bears the date of 1331.

Der Pfaffenwinkel im Morgennebel

The Pfaffenwinkel in the morning fog

Sehenswert sind die drei Rokoko-Altäre, die man aus der 1803 aufgelösten Stiftskirche von Rottenbuch erwarb und teilweise durch Schnitzfiguren ergänzte, sowie die qualitätvollen Beichtstühle und die Kanzel. Für den Hauptaltar, der den gesamten Innenraum der Kirche beherrscht und dennoch in Rottenbuch Seitenaltar war, musste man das Chorgewölbe anheben. Er ist ebenso wie die Seitenfiguren ein Werk Franz Xaver Schmädls von 1758. Die monumentale Krypta, das ehemalige Beinhaus, entstand vor 1350.

Nur etwa 700 m vom Ortskern entfernt steht die **Wallfahrtskirche** Maria Egg (um 1700), die durch ihre reiche Ausstattung gefällt. In ihrem Anbau hat man das „Museum am Klösterle" liebevoll eingerichtet.

The three rococo altars are worth looking at; they were acquired in 1803 from the monastery church of Rottenbuch when this was dissolved, and were partly decorated with carved figures. To accommodate the High Altar, which dominates the entire interior of the church even though in Rottenbuch it was only a side altar, it was necessary to raise the whole vault of the Choir. This, as well as the flanking sculptures, were made by Franz Xaver Schmädel in 1758. The monumental crypt, formerly an ossuary, was built before 1350.

Only about 700 metres from the centre is the **pilgrimage church** of Maria Egg (about 1700), the appeal of which is its relatively rich interior. Next to it we can find the **"Museum am Klösterle"**.

Rottenbuch

Schon von weitem grüßt der seitlich vom Kirchenschiff abgesetzte Turm des einstigen **Augustiner-Chorherrenstifts**, hervorgegangen aus einem von Herzog Welf I. 1073 gestifteten Kloster. Nach Zerstörungen im Mittelalter entstanden um 1700 und um 1750 neue, prächtige Klostergebäude, die jedoch im Zuge der Säkularisation 1803 weitgehend abgebrochen wurden. Äußerlich schlicht gehalten, überzeugt das Gotteshaus durch eine perfekte Harmonie der drei Stilarten Romanik, Gotik und Barock. Während von der ersten Bauepoche um 1100 im Wesentlichen nur der für diese Gegend ungewöhnliche Grundbau mit dem Querschiff erhalten blieb, entstammt der Aufbau von Kirchenschiff und Turm dem 15. Jahrhundert. Aber erst die Rokoko-Ausstattung im 18. Jahrhundert gab der Kirche vor allem durch die üppige Stuckierung von J. Schmuzer und Sohn sowie die schönen Fresken des Matthäus Günther ihr heutiges Aussehen. Ergänzt wird diese raumumfassende Pracht von der trotz der Veräußerungen von 1803 wertvollen Ausstattung vor allem durch Franz Xaver Schmädl, der um 1760 neben zahllosen Engelsfiguren u.a. den Orgelsprospekt, die Kanzel, die vier erhaltenen Seitenaltäre, die Stifterfiguren sowie den herrlichen Hochaltar schuf. Ein besonderes Kleinod der gotischen Sakralkunst enthält der – vom Chor aus – erste Seitenaltar rechts: eine qualitätvolle spätgotische Madonna (um 1483), die ihrem Kind eine Frucht reicht.

Rottenbuch

The tower of the **former Augustine monastery**, offset from the nave of its church, greets from a long way off. This monastery is the successor to an earlier one, founded in 1073 by Duke Welf I but destroyed during the course of the Middle Ages. Around 1700, and later in about 1750, this magnificent new monastery building arose but work on it ceased abruptly in 1803 when the monasteries were dissolved and „secularised". Plain and simple on the outside, the church shows a convincing harmony of Roman, gothic, and baroque styles. Whilst the only remnants of the first stage of building of about 1100 are the foundations and the crossing, which are unusual for this region, the superstructure of nave and tower date from the 15th century. The church's present day appearance really only dates from 18th century, with in particular the luxuriant stucco work of J. Schmuzer and his son and the beautiful frescoes of Matthäus Günther. The lush magnificence of the Franz Xaver Schmädl interior (about 1750), which still inundates the interior despite the forced sale of the building in 1803, is augmented particularly by the numerous figures of angels, the organ case, the pulpit, the four side-altars, the figures of the founders, and the magnificent High Altar which he created. One special jewel of Gothic church art can be seen in the first side-altar on the right, when seen from the Choir; a valuable late-Gothic Madonna (about 1483), handing fruit to the Christ-child.

Der Klosterkomplex von Rottenbuch mit der Klosterkirche

The monastery complex of Rottenbuch with its central church

Die prächtige gotische Klosterkirche mit herrlichen
Fresken und Engelsfiguren im Stil des Rokoko

*The magnificent Gothic monastery church with its
gorgeous frescoes and angels in the rococo style*

Wildsteig

Durch seine Lage inmitten von Natur- und Landschafts-schutzgebieten mit seltenen Pflanzen und Tieren ist Wild-steig als Erholungsort anerkannt.

Das ansprechende Gotteshaus, **St. Jakob** geweiht, erhielt seine heutige Gestalt in der zweiten Hälfte des 18. Jahr-hunderts. Außen denkbar bescheiden gehalten, gefällt die Kirche durch ihren hellen, heiter wirkenden Innenraum. Die feinen Stuckierungen des Wessobrunner Meisters Thassilo Zöpf und seines Schülers Doll zeigen Merkmale sowohl des Barock als auch des weit strengeren Klassizis-mus. Die qualitätvollen Fresken malte der Oberammer-gauer Künstler Franz S. Zwinck, den man nach seinem Hausnamen „Lüftlmaler" nannte. Bemerkenswert ist auch der Hochaltar mit einem Bild des Malers Johann Degler (1666-1729) und den beiden hervorragenden spätgo-tischen Begleitfiguren, die einst den gotischen Hochaltar der Klosterkirche in Rottenbuch zierten.

Wildsteig

Wildsteig is recognised as a healthy holiday area becau-se of its position in the middle of a protected-landscape area with its rare plants and animals.

The attractive church, dedicated to **St Jacob**, was given its present shape in the second half of the 18th century. Outwardly as plain and modest as can be, the church's appealing feature is its light, friendly interior. The fine stucco work by the Wessobrunn master Thassilo Zöpf and his pupil Doll display features both of baroque and of classicism. The high-quality frescoes were painted by the Oberammergau artist Franz S. Zwinck, who earned himself the nickname of Luftmaler – an artist who paints with air. The High Altar is also worthy of note, with a picture by the painter Johann Degler (1666-1729), and the two outstanding late-Gothic accompanying figures which once decorated the Gothic High Altar in the mo-nastery church in Rottenbuch.

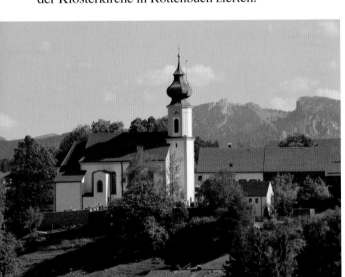

Wieskirche und Steingaden

Wieskirche and Steingaden

Ihrem Namen Ehre machend, taucht die schlichte, weiße Kirche inmitten der Wiesen und vor dem dunklen Hintergrund der Berge auf. Wie kommt ein so herrliches Gotteshaus in diese Einsamkeit der Wälder, Wiesen und Hochmoore? Im Jahr 1730 hatten zwei Prämonstratenserpater des Klosters Steingaden für die Karfreitagsprozession aus verschiedenen Holzfiguren einen „Gegeißelten Heiland" gefertigt. Seine Gelenke überzogen sie mit Leinwand, die sie mit roter Farbe bemalten. Mancher nahm Anstoß an der allzu „blutbefleckten" Statue, die daraufhin 1734 auf dem Dachboden eines

The full name is „Pilgrimage Church to Our Tortured Saviour on the Meadow", and suitably enough it appears as a plain, white church surrounded by meadows and in front of the dark backdrop of the mountains. What is such a magnificent church doing in the lonely midst of the forests and meadows and marshes? In 1730, two priests of the Prémont order, from the monastery of Steingaden, had prepared a „Tortured Saviour" from various wooden figures for the Good Friday procession. They covered the limbs of their figure with linen and painted it with red paint. Many people were upset

Die barocke Wieskirche im Einklang zwischen Natur und Architektur

The baroque Wieskirche in harmony between nature and architecture

Gastwirts in Steingaden verschwand. Bereits vier Jahre später holte sich eine Verwandte des Wirts die Figur auf ihren „Wieshof" und verehrte sie hoch. Noch im selben Jahr geschah das „Wunder in der Wies", als man auf dem Antlitz des „Gegeißelten Heilands" Tränen entdeckte.

by the statue, as it seemed to be too heavily „bloodstained", and in 1734 it disappeared into the loft of an inn-keeper in Steingaden. Only four years later, a relative of the innkeeper took the figure away to her Wieshof, her „farm in the meadows", and held it in the

Sogleich setzte eine starke Wallfahrtsbewegung ein, die fromme Pilger selbst aus der Schweiz, Böhmen, Tirol und Ungarn zu der 1740 erbauten Feldkapelle führte. Bei dem weiter wachsenden Ansturm entschloss sich der Abt von Steingaden bereits 1745, hier eine große **Wallfahrtskirche** zu erbauen. Dem Wessobrunner Baumeister Dominikus Zimmermann, damals bereits 60 Jahre alt, gelang mit der weltberühmten Wieskirche die Krone seines künstlerischen Schaffens. Der Bruder des Baumeisters, Johann Baptist Zimmermann, Hofmaler am kurfürstlichen Hof in München, schuf die viel bewunderten Deckenfresken, wohl mit die schönsten Werke der Rokokomalerei. Anton Sturm und Aegidius Verhelst arbeiteten als Bildhauer. Der säulenumrahmte **Hochaltar** beherrscht den Chor und birgt das berühmte Gnadenbild. Die Säulen hier wirken wie Marmor, sind jedoch aus Stuck gefertigt, so dass sie farblich nach dem Plan des Architekten gestaltet werden konnten. Das scheinbare Steingewölbe des Langhauses, 28 m lang und 18 m breit, ließ D. Zimmermann in Holz fertigen.

greatest reverence, and it was in this same year that the „miracle of the meadows" happened; tears were seen on the face of the „Tortured Saviour". A surge of pilgrims travelled even from Switzerland, Bohemia, the Tyrol, and Hungary to the field chapel, built in 1740. As the flood of pilgrims increased still further, the Abbot of Steingaden decided in 1745 to build a large **pilgrimage church** here. The Wessobrunn architect Dominikus Zimmermann, already 60 years old, succeeded in setting the crowning glory on his artistic creation by building the world-famous Wieskirche. His brother, Johann Baptist Zimmermann, court painter at the court of the Princes Elector in Munich, created the much admired ceiling frescoes with works that must surely be amongst the most beautiful of all rococo painting. Anton Sturm and Aegidius Verhelst worked as sculptors. The **High Altar**, framed with columns, dominates the Choir and houses the famous Picture of Grace. The columns here look like marble but were in fact made of stucco, so that they could blend in with the architect's plan. The vaulted

Wieskirche: Eine überwältigende Schönheit

Wieskirche: An overwhelming beauty

Das Münster von Steingaden

The minster of Steingaden

Der säulenumrahmte Hochaltar

With pillars surronded high altar

Die **Decke** ist, bis auf eine Hohlkehle von etwa 2,50 m, völlig flach, wirkt jedoch durch die perspektivischen Malereien und die raffinierte Farbgebung wie ein echtes Gewölbe über dem Oval des Langhauses. Dieses ist nach Westen hin noch einmal ausgebuchtet, um Raum für die anmutig geschwungene Orgelempore zu schaffen, eine Augenweide in Weiß und Gold.

Vor seinem Aufbruch zum 2. Kreuzzug gründete Herzog Welf VI. im heutigen Erholungsort Steingaden 1147 das **Prämonstratenserkloster**, das bis 1803 existierte. Die romanische Fassade des Münsters repräsentiert den Baustil in der Zeit der Ordensgründung, die qualitätvolle Ausstattung die Stilepochen der Jahrhunderte bis zur Auflösung des Klosters. Neben dem Münster, das zur Pfarrkirche des Ortes wurde, sind von den einst umfangreichen Baulichkeiten der westliche Flügel des stimmungsvollen **romanischen Kreuzgangs** (13. Jh., gotisches Gewölbe), die **Brunnenkapelle** (15 Jh.) und die **Johanneskapelle** (12. Jh.) erhalten.

Romanischer Kreuzgang des einzigsten Klosters

West wing of the former cloister

roof, 28 metres long and 18 wide, which looks like masonry, was in fact produced in wood to Dominikus Zimmermann's design. The **ceiling** is completely flat, except for a cavetto of about 2.50 metres, but because of the perspective painting and sophisticated colouring looks like a genuine vault above the oval shape of the nave. This curves out again towards the west, to create sufficient space for a gracefully curved organ loft, a treat for the eyes in white and gold.

Before setting off on the Second Crusade, Duke Welf VI founded the **Prémont monastery** here in 1147, which remained in existence until 1803. The Roman-style facade of the minster represents the architectural style of the time when the Order was founded. In addition to the minster, which became the parish church of the little town, the only parts remaining of what was once an extensive complex of buildings are the west wing of the **cloister** (13th century, Gothic vaulted roof), the **Brunnenkapelle** (15th century), and **St John's chapel**.

Halblech

Weit verstreut liegen die Ortsteile mit ihren insgesamt 3500 Einwohnern in naturschöner Landschaft zwischen dem Ammergebirge und dem Lechtal mit seinen zahlreichen Seen. Das verspricht ein urgemütliches Feriengebiet in ländlicher Abgeschiedenheit, das dennoch verkehrsgünstig zwischen den touristischen Highlights Steingaden/Wieskirche und Füssen/Königsschlösser liegt. Ideal ist der Ort mit seinen zahlreichen **Freizeitmöglichkeiten** ebenso für Wanderer und Naturliebhaber.

Halblech

The villages and their 3500 inhabitants are scattered across the beautiful natural landscape between the Ammergebirge and the Lech Valley with its numerous lakes. This allows to spend extremely relaxing holidays in total seclusion that still ensures convenient access to the main tourist attractions of Steingaden/Wieskirche and Füssen/royal castles. Numerous **recreational opportunities** also make the place ideal for hikers and wildlife enthusiasts.

Traumhafte Allgäu-Landschaft um Halblech

Dreamlike Allgäu landscape around Halblech

Schwangau
mit den Königsschlössern

Malerisch steht auf grüner Wiese die hübsche **Wallfahrtskirche** St. Coloman (1673). Ebenso wie bei ihrem Schwesterbau „Mariae Heimsuchung" in Ilgen war Johann Schmuzer hier Architekt und Stuckateur. Die Kirche besitzt einige sehenswerte spätgotische Schnitzwerke. Sie wurde nach einem irischen Pilger benannt, der hier rastete und heute als Schutzpatron des Viehs gilt. Ihm zu Ehren findet in Schwangau alljährlich der Colomansritt statt und am 26. Mai, am „Wurmfeiertag", ein Bittgang zur Kirche: Die gläubige Bevölkerung hatte das einst versprochen, wenn der Heilige sie von der herrschenden Engerlingsplage befreite.

Schwangau
and the Royal Castles

The pretty **pilgrimage church of St Coloman** (1673) stands in the middle of a green meadow. Like its sister building, the Mariae Heimsuchung in Ilgen, the architect and stucco-master here was Johann Schmuzer. This church possesses notable late-Gothic carvings, and was named after an Irish pilgrim who rested here and is now honoured as the patron saint of farm animals; the Colomansritt takes place in Schwangau every year, and on 26th May, which is Wurmfeiertag or worms' holiday, there is a procession of petition to the church; the pious populace originally undertook to do this if the saint would relieve them of a plague of cock-chafers.

Die Wallfahrtskirche St. Coloman, im Hintergrund Schloss Neuschwanstein vor den ersten Alpengipfeln

The pilgrimage church of St. Coloman, with the Castle of Neuschwanstein in the background

93

Von hier aus sieht man bereits das strahlend weiße Schloss **Neuschwanstein**, das einer phantastischen Theaterkulisse zu entstammen scheint. Es handelt sich hier um die geistige Schöpfung des Märchenkönigs Ludwig II. von Bayern, der 1864 als Achtzehnjähriger den

From here one can already see the brilliant white spectacle of Castle **Neuschwanstein**, one of the most fantastic and theatrical of all scenes. This is the intellectual creation of the mad King Ludwig II of Bavaria, known as the Märchenkönig or Fairy-Tale King, who came

Schloss Neuschwanstein: Traumschloss König Ludwigs II. von Bayern

Castle of Neuschwanstein: Dreamlike castle of King Ludwig II. of Bavaria

Thron bestieg. Der schöne und einsame Monarch war begeistert von der germanischen Sagenwelt, die ihm die Musikdramen Richard Wagners nahe gebracht hatten. Er zog sich mehr und mehr in eine Traumwelt zurück, zu der auch seine Schlossbauten in Neuschwanstein, Linderhof und Herrenchiemsee gehörten, Meisterwerke Stein gewordener Vergangenheit. Sein tragischer und bis heute ungeklärter Tod im Starnberger See beendete abrupt seine Bautätigkeit.

Schloss Neuschwanstein ließ er ab 1869 nach dem Vorbild der Wartburg in der Nähe des Alpsees auf einem wildromantischen Felsen über dem Wasserfall der Pöllatschlucht erbauen. In romanischem Stil entstand ein fünfstöckiger Palas, reich verziert mit schlanken Türmen und Söllern. Die prunkvollen Wohn- und Repräsentationsräume zeigen in ihrer bildnerischen Ausgestaltung fast ausschließlich Motive aus der deutschen Vorzeit mit den Sagengestalten des Siegfried und Lohengrin, des Tannhäuser und Parzifal sowie Darstellungen des sagenhaften Sängerwettstreits und der Meistersinger. Eine Steigerung der überreich geschmückten Räume

to the throne in 1864 at the age of 18. A good-looking but lonely monarch, he was enthralled by the world of German sagas and legends to which the musical dramas of Richard Wagner had introduced him. He withdrew ever further into his dream world, to which the castles also belonged which he built: Neuschwanstein, Lindenhof, and Herrenchiemsee: masterpieces of past history turned into stone. His tragic death in the Starnberger See, still to this day a mystery, put an abrupt end to his architectural efforts.

He ordered Neuschwanstein to be built from 1869 onwards, taking the Wartburg (in Saxony) as his prototype and setting it, a five-storied palace, on a wild, romantic cliff above the Alpsee and the Pöllatschlucht waterfall and decorating it richly with lofty rooms and slender towers. The magnificent residential and formal rooms are decorated almost exclusively with pictures and symbols from German pre-history, with the legendary figures of Siegfried and Lohengrin, Tannhäuser and Parzifal, and illustrations of the fabled singers' competition and the Meistersinger. The King exceeded himself in these

Neuschwanstein: Thronsaal   *Neuschwanstein: Throne room*

Schloss Neuschwanstein: Wohnzimmer des Königs

Living room of the king

Altar der Hauskapelle

The altar of the castle chapel

gelang dem Bauherrn mit dem Sängersaal, der die gesamte Länge des 4. Stockwerks einnimmt und dem Sängersaal auf der Wartburg nachempfunden ist. Vom westlich vorgelagerten Söller bietet sich dem Besucher ein herrlicher Ausblick über das Ammergebirge und die Tannheimer Berge.

Sehenswert ist auch die eiserne Marienbrücke, die in 92 m Höhe über die Schlucht führt und eine schöne **Aussicht** auf den 45 Meter tiefen Wasserfall ermöglicht. Weniger hoch liegen die gelben Gebäude des **Schlosses Hohenschwangau** auf einem bewaldeten Hügel. Hier stand einst die Stammburg der Herren von Schwangau, die der Vater König Ludwigs II., Maximilian II., im neugotischen Tudorstil einer englischen Burg wieder aufbauen ließ. Auch hier erinnert der Schwanenrittersaal an die Lohengrin-Sage, hier machte der junge Ludwig II. erste Bekanntschaft mit dem Sagengut, das seine Welt werden sollte. Vom Balkon des Tasso-Zimmers beobachtete Ludwig später mit dem Fernrohr die Fortschritte beim Bau von Neuschwanstein.

Größter und prächtigster Saal von Neuschwanstein: der Sängersaal

extravagantly decorated rooms with the Sängersaal or Singers' Room, which takes up the entire length of the fourth floor and is a copy of Tannhäuser's legendary castle. From the western side the visitor can enjoy a magnificent view across the Upper Bavarian landscape of mountains and lakes.

The sights worth seeing at the top include the iron Marienbrücke, which leads across the gorge at a height of 92 metres and provides a wonderful **view** of the 45-metre high waterfall. The yellow buildings of **Castle Hohenschwangau** stand at a lower point on a wooded hill. This is where the Lords of Schwangau once had their family residence, built by Ludwig II's father, Maximilian II, in the neo-Gothic Tudor style of an English castle. Here again, the Schwanenrittersaal (the „hall of the knights of the swan") is evocative of the Lohengrin legend, and this is where the young Ludwig II made his first acquaintance with the heritage of legends and sagas which were to become his world.

The biggest and most gorgeous hall of Neuschwanstein: the singer's hall

**Schloss
Hohenschwangau**

*Castle
Hohenschwangau*

**Hohenschwangau:
Ritterzimmer**

*Castle
Hohenschwangau:
knight's room*

Blick über Neuschwanstein in die weite Ebene des östlichen Allgäu

View over Neuschwanstein to the wide layer of the east of Allgäu

Bei schönem Wetter empfiehlt sich die Fahrt mit der Kabinenseilbahn auf den **Tegelberg** (1730 m), einen hervorragenden Aussichtspunkt über die Alpenmassive und Ausgangspunkt für Wanderungen durch das Naturschutzgebiet Ammergebirge. Der malerische heilklimatische Kurort Schwangau (3400 Einwohner) bietet neben seinen Schlössern die Ebene am Forggensee, grüne Hügel und schroffe Alpengipfel, aber auch vier Seen und einen unverfälschten Ortskern.

In fine weather it is worth taking the cable car up the **Tegelberg** (1730 metres), an outstanding viewing-point from which one can see whole of the Alps and also an excellent start-point for walking tours through the Ammergebirge nature conservancy area. The centre of the holiday resort of Schwangau (population: 3,400), apart from the castles offers the plain around the Forggensee, green hills, and rugged Alpine peaks, not forgetting the four lakes and an unspoilt, authentic town centre.

Füssen

Die Allgäuer Alpen formte die Kraft des Lechgletschers in der letzten Eiszeit, eine liebliche Landschaft mit Moränenhügeln und zahlreichen Seen. Um die Zeitenwende eroberten die Römer das Gebiet, erschlossen es mit einer Militärstraße, der Via Claudia Augusta (Venedig-Augsburg), und sicherten den Zugang zum Pass durch ein Kastell auf dem heutigen Schlossberg. Im 8. Jahrhundert wirkte der hl. Magnus als Missionar und Lehrer des Glaubens in Füssen, wo er um 750 starb. Aus seiner Zelle entwickelte sich im Laufe der Jahrhunderte das heutige St.-Mang-Kloster mit der Basilika, in deren Krypta sich ein Fresco (um 980) befindet, das die Heiligen Magnus und Gallus darstellt. Im Jahre 1313 geriet die Stadt unter die Oberhoheit des Fürstbischofs von Augsburg, ehe sie 1802 an Bayern fiel. Aus der ehemaligen römischen Nachschubstraße hatte sich im Mittelalter eine wichtige Handelsstraße entwickelt mit Füssen als Umschlagplatz, wo die Waren aus Italien auf Flöße umgeladen wurden. An der Blüte der Stadt im 15. Jahrhundert hatten auch die ansässigen Handwerker ihren Anteil, unter denen vor allem die Lauten- und später die Geigenmacher internationale Bedeutung erlangten.

Blick über den Lech auf das Kloster St. Mang, darüber das Hohe Schloss

Füssen

At the foot of the Allgäu Alps ,the force of the Lech glacier in the last Ice Age created a charming landcape of moraine hills and numerous lakes. At about the time of Christ's birth, Romans conquered this area and opened it up with a military road, the via claudia (from Venice to Augsburg), securing the access to the pass with a castella (fort) on the hill now called the Schlossberg. In the 8th century, St Magnus worked as a missionary and teacher of the Faith in Füssen, where he died in 750. His monkish cell gradually developed over the centuries into the present-day St Mang's monastery with its church, in the crypt of which there is a fresco (about 980) representing St Magnus and St Gallus. In 1313, the town came under the sovereignty of the Prince-Bishops of Augsburg, and was then annexed to Bavaria in 1802. The former Roman military supply road had by the Middle Ages become an important trading route, and Füssen a transshipment point at which goods from Italy were loaded onto rafts. During the town`s highest floweringin the 15th century, the local craftsman also profited from this trade, with the makers of lutes and later also of violins enjoying an international reputation.

View across the River Lech to the St. Mang's church, with the High Castle above it

Die Reichenstraße mit dem Kirchturm von St. Mang (li.) und dem Uhrturm des Hohen Schlosses

The Reichenstraße with St Mang's church tower (left) and the clock tower

Heute ist Füssen (14000 Einwohner), der Glanzpunkt des Ostallgäus, ein attraktiver Urlaubs- und Kurort mit einer Fülle von Freizeitmöglichkeiten zu jeder Jahreszeit. Vom Kaiser-Maximilian-Platz führt die **Reichenstraße** mitten in die Altstadt. Hier wohnten die Händler und Handwerker, die der Straße den Namen gaben. Über die Fassaden der Reichenstraße blickt der Uhrenturm des **Hohen Schlosses**. Erbaut von 1291 bis 1503, diente es als Sommerresidenz der Augsburger Fürstbischöfe. Zwei Erker zieren den **Uhrenturm**: Der eine konnte

Füssen today , with its 16,400 inhabitants, is the shining star of the eastern Allgäu , and a central tourist location with a huge number of leisure activities at all times of the year. From here the **Reichenstrasse** leads through the middle of the old town centre, where the traders and craftsmen lived who gave the street its name: „Rich people's street". The clock tower of the **Hohes Schloss** looks down across the façades of the Reichenstrasse. Built between 1291 and 1503, this castle served as the summer residence of the Prince-Bishops of Augsburg.

105

als Gusserker zur Verteidigung des Schlosses genutzt werden, der über Eck gestellte diente als Ausguck für den Türmer, der aufkommende nächtliche Feuer melden musste. Wo sich die Reichenstraße marktähnlich verbreitert, erinnert links am ehemaligen Zächerlhaus eine eiserne Kanonenkugel an die Beschießung der Stadt am 11.7.1800 durch Napoleons Truppen. Nach dem Durchschreiten des äußeren Schlosstors haben wir den romantischen „Malerwinkel" erreicht, in dem zwei

Das Hohe Schloss

The **clock tower** is graced by two oriole windows, one of which could be used for pouring unpleasant material onto the heads of anyone attacking the castle; the other, mounted across the corner, was a look-out point for the tower watchmen who had to sound a warning if fire broke out at night. At the point where the Reichenstrasse widens out and looks like a market street there is an iron cannon ball in the wall of the former Zächerlhaus as a reminder of the day – it was 11th June

The High castle

Blick vom Schlossaufgang zum Turm der Klosterkirche

View from the castle rise to the tower of the monastery church

Durchfahrten, der Wehrgang und ein spitzbehelmter Wehrturm den Betrachter begeistern. Zwischen den Fenstern des Obergeschosses erkennen wir die Wappen des Hochstifts Augsburg (rot-weiß) und des Bauherrn Friedrich von Zollern (um 1500). Aus dieser Zeit ist auch die kunstvolle gotische Kassettendecke im Rittersaal erhalten. Vom Hohen Schloss genießen wir den Ausblick über den Lech und die Alpenberge. Zu unseren Füßen liegen die Baulichkeiten des ehemaligen **Benediktinerstifts St. Mang**, dessen Kirchenbau (1701-17) der einheimische Baumeister Herkomer leitete.

Ähnlich wie beim Hohen Schloss verzierte man um 1500 den romanischen Kirchturm mit Illusionsmalerei. Im Innern gefallen die reizenden Engelsgestalten (1719) des Anton Sturm sowie die stimmungsvolle Krypta, die noch von der romanischen Vorgängerkirche übrig blieb. Dort unten entdeckte man 1950 ein Fresko, das

1800 – when Napoleon's troops bombarded the town. The romantic „painters' corner" has two particularly attractive sights: the sally port and a defensive tower with a pointed cupola. There is another fantastic view from the gate-tower room on the gable side of the north wing, which is adjoined by the Dreifaltigkeitsturm. Between the windows of the upper floor we can see the red-and-white coat-ofarms of Augsburg and of the builder of the castle (in about 1500), Friedrich von Zollern. The artistic Gothic cassetted ceiling in the Rittersaal dates from the same time. The historically important rooms, however, now house the **municipal museum of Füssen**, and these include St Anna's chapel; here one can see the oldest representation of the **Dance of Death** anywhere in Bavaria, painted in 1602 by Jakob Hiebeler. The vistor reaches the courtyard of the town hall and thus the musem from the Lechhalde side, where the busts of

St.-Anna-Kapelle: „Totentanz" von Jakob Hiebeler

St. Anna's chapel: Jakob Hiebeler's „Dance of Death"

Museum der Stadt Füssen: Klosterbibliothek

Füssen municipal museum: the monastery library

mit der Krypta vor dem Jahr 1000 entstanden war und teilweise recht gut erhalten ist. Etwa 200 Jahre jünger ist die umfangreiche Freskenfolge im Kreuzgang des Klosters, das heute großenteils als Rathaus dient. Die historisch bedeutsamsten Räume jedoch beherbergen

the four great benefactors of the monastery decorate the narrow entrance: Charles the Strong, Pippin, Leopold of Austria, and Welf of Swabia. The showpiece of the present-day town hall is the magnificently painted and stuccoed **Fürstensaal**, in which concerts are held in the

**Wandern am ->
Schwansee**

*Hiking at the ->
Schwansee*

**Rokokofassade
der Heilig-Geist-
Spitalkirche**

*Front facade of the
Heilig-Geist-Spital
church*

heute das **Museum der Stadt Füssen**. Dazu gehört die St.-Anna-Kapelle, in der sich die älteste Darstellung eines **Totentanzes** in Bayern befindet, gemalt 1602 von Jakob Hiebeler. Rathaushof und Museum erreicht der Besucher von der Lechhalde aus, wo die Büsten der vier Wohltäter des Klosters – Karl der Große, Pippin, Leopold von Österreich und Welf von Schwaben – die enge Tordurchfahrt zieren. Schmuckstück des heutigen Rathauses ist der herrlich ausgemalte und stuckierte **Fürstensaal**, in dem im Sommer Konzerte stattfinden. Unterhalb des Schlosses gefällt die schmucke **Spital-kirche** (1748/49), die eine reiche barocke Innenausstattung besitzt. Dieses Juwel des schwäbisch-bayerischen Rokoko schuf der einheimische Baumeister Franz Karl Fischer. Gegenüber erinnert eine Gedenktafel an das ehemalige Lechtor. Von drüben hat man einen schönen Blick über den Lech und die Altstadtdächer auf das Kloster und das Hohe Schloss. Füssen ist nicht nur historische Altstadt, es lebt von und mit seiner herrlichen Landschaft. Zu Füssen gehören der Weißensee mit dem gleichnamigen Luftkurort und der Hopfensee mit dem Kneippkurort **Hopfen am See**, an einem Sonnenhang über dem Gewässer gelegen. An beiden Seen ist Rudern, Segeln, Surfen, Baden und Angeln ebenso gut möglich wie am 16 km² großen **Forggensee**. Zusammen mit den kleineren Gewässern besitzt Füssen allein zehn Seen und ist daher im Sommer ebenso ein Anziehungspunkt für Wasserfreunde wie im Winter für Liebhaber von Aktivitäten auf dem Eis oder im Schnee.

summer. The fine **Spitalkirche** (1748-49) on the left, which possesses a rich baroque interior. This jewel of Swabian-Bavarian rococo was created by a local architect, Franz Karl Fischer. Opposite there is a plaque commemorating the former Lechtor, the gateway on the river side, and from where there is a fine view across the river and the roofs of the old town centre with the monastery and the castle in the background. From here the Tiroler Strasse leads to the suburb of **Ziegelwies**, on the Austrian border, and a good starting-point for walks to the royal castles (2.5 kilometres), to the legendary Schwansee, to the Alpsee which Ludwig II particularly loved, or to the Kalvarienberg with the neo-Gothic chapel to the Virgin Mary. Füssen is not only a historic old town; it lives from and with its magnificent landscape. The road westwards leads to the outlying villages of **Bad Faulenbach**, acknowledged as a curative spa with mineral and mud baths, and **Weissensee**, a picturesque resort on the banks of the eponymous lake. The other lake, the Hopfensee, is approximately the same size and boasts the spa resort of **Hopfen am See**, lying on a sunny slope above the water. Both lakes offer facilities for rowing, sailing, surfing, swimming, and fishing, as does the **Forggensee**, an artificial lake of 16 square kilometres created by damming the Lech. Together with the smaller lakes, Füssen alone has a total of ten lakes and is thus just as much an attraction in the summer for lovers of water sports as it is in the winter for those who love ice and snow.

Die Zugspitze

Deutschlands höchster Berg (2962 m) gehört zum Wettersteingebirge ist bis etwa 1800 m ü. M. von Wald bedeckt. Die schroffen Wände, scharfen Grate und Gipfel bestehen überwiegend aus hellem Wettersteinkalk, der sich im Erdmittelalter im Meer ablagerte und heute an der Nordseite der Zugspitze eine über 2200 m hohe Felswand bildet, eine der gewaltigsten der Ostalpen. Unterhalb der Zugspitze liegen zwei der insgesamt drei kleinen Gletscher der deutschen Alpen. Beide sind vom Gipfel aus gut zu sehen.

Über das Reintal und die Knorrhütte führt seit 1873 ein Fußweg auf die Zugspitze. Für den Weg von Garmisch sollten Sie mindestens 10 Stunden reine Gehzeit einplanen sowie schwindelfrei und trittsicher sein. Seit 1930 kann der Besucher den Höhenunterschied von 1950 m zum Schneefernerhaus mittels Zahnradbahn mühelos überwinden. Die 11 km lange Fahrt von Grainau durch Wald, Felsen und Tunnel, mit Zusteigemöglichkeit am Eibsee (972 m), ist noch heute ein Erlebnis. Vom Eibsee führt seit 1963 eine Großkabinenbahn direkt auf den Gipfel.

Zugspitze

Germany's highest mountain (2962 m) belongs to the Wetterstein chain and it is covered by forests up to about 1800 metres above sea level. Its steep walls, its sharp ridges and peaks are mainly made of light limestone which deposited in the sea during the Mesozoic Era and which today forms a more than 2200 metres high rock-face on the northern side of Mount Zugspitze, one of most imposing faces of the Eastern Alps. Below Zugspitze there are two of the three small glaciers to be found in the German Alps. Both of them can be seen from the top of the Zugspitze.

Since 1873 a **footpath** leads to Zugspitze passing through Reintal and past Knorrhütte. For the path from Garmisch you have to calculate at least 10 hours' walk, have a good head for heights and a steady step. Since 1930, the 1950 m height difference as far as Schneefernerhaus can be overcome without any problems thanks to the **rack-railway**. The 11 kilometres from Grainau through forests, rocks and tunnels, with the possibility to get on at Eibsee (972 m), are an unforgettable experience still today. From Lake Eibsee, since 1963 a **carway**

Von hier aus ist der Rundblick an klaren Tagen über-
wältigend – die Sichtweite beträgt dann rund 200 km zu
den Bergriesen Österreichs, der Schweiz und Italiens.
Der Gipfel selbst ist allerdings fast vollständig zuge-
baut, lediglich ein mit Drahtseil gesicherter Klettersteig
ermöglicht – für Schwindelfreie – den Aufstieg zum
Gipfelkreuz. Ein grenzüberschreitender kurzer Spaziergang führt zur Bergstation der Tiroler Zugspitzbahn.
Auf dem Zugspitzplatt sind eine Wanderung zum Gletscher (ca. ½ Stunde) und ein Besuch der Kapelle „Mariä
Himmelfahrt" zu empfehlen.
Weitaus mehr ursprüngliche Natur findet der Wanderer
und Spaziergänger rund um die Alpspitze (2050 m),
die mit der Alpspitzbahn erschlossen ist. Restaurants,
ein Klettergarten, beschilderte Wanderwege und ein
Lehrpfad hinab zum Kreuzeck(1651 m) bieten viel-
fache Möglichkeiten. Von Kreuzeck führt eine weitere
Kabinenbahn hinunter ins Tal.
Als familienfreundlicher Sonnenberg gilt der Wank
(1780 m), der mit viersitzigen Gondeln erschlossen ist.

leads directly to the top. From here you can enjoy an
extraordinary panorama on clear days, when the visi-
bility reaches up to 200 kilometres as far as Austrian,
Swiss and Italian mountains. On the contrary, the top
is closed from almost every side and you can climb to
the cross only thanks to a wire-cable, at least if do not
feel dizzy! A small walk brings to the other side of the
border to the Tyrolese railway station.
On **Zugspitze plateau** we recommend a walk to the
glacier (about ½ hour) and to the chapel of Our Lady
of the Assumption.
The ones who love walking and hiking can find a more
intact nature on Mount Alpspitze (2050 metres), to be
reached by the **Alpspitze railway**. A wide range of
possibilities are offered thanks to restaurants, climbing
wall, marked hiking paths and a didactic itinerary to
Mount Kreuzeck (1651 m). From Kreuzeck you can go
down to the valley by **carway**.
A four-seated gondola-way brings to **Mount Wank**
(1780 m), the « sunny » mountain, most preferred by
families.

© **Willi Sauer Verlag**
Mühlhausener Straße 25 · **69234 Dielheim**
Tel. 06222/72084 · Fax: 664813
E-Mail: willi.v.sauer@t-online.de
Text: Wolfgang Kootz, Bammental
Druck: Kraft Druck GmbH
Satz: Michaela Schweiß
Gestaltung: Willi Sauer
Übersetzungen: Anita Sauer

Wir bedanken uns herzlich für die freundliche Unterstützung bei der
Arbeitsgemeinschaft Romantische Straße
91550 Dinkelsbühl, Segringer Straße 10
Tel. +49(0)9851/551387
E-Mail: info@romantischestrasse.de

Bildnachweis:
Mit freundlicher Unterstützung:
Touristik-Arbeitsgemeinschaft Romantische Straße: Umschlagseite; 2, 3, 4; Congress-Tourismus-Wirtschaft-Würzburg: S. 6, 7; Wertheim-Village: S. 11; Tourist-Information Tauberbischofsheim: S. 12, 13, 14, 15; Kultur-Verkehrsamt Lauda-Königshofen: S. 17; Tourist Information Kultur-und Verkehrsamt Weikersheim S. 24; Bad Mergentheim S. 19, 20; Kapellenpflege „Stuppacher Madonna"; Verkehrsamt Röttingen: S. 26; Tourist-Information Creglingen: S. 27; Fingerhutmuseum: S. 29; Städt. Verkehrsamt Schillingsfürst S. 40; Tourist-Information Feuchtwangen: S. 43; Touristik-Service Dinkelsbühl: S. 46, 47, 49; Tourist-Information Nördlingen im Ries: S. 52, 55, 56; Rieskratermuseum S. 55; Städtische Tourist-Information Donauwörth: S. 60, 61, 63; Stadt Rain Umschlagseite 4; Regio Augsburg Tourismus GmbH S. 66, 69, 70, 72, 73; Fremdenverkehrsbüro Friedberg S. 74, 75; Kultur-u.Fremdenverkehrsamt Landsberg am Lech: S. 76, 77; Tourismusverband Pfaffenwinkel-Schongau S. 85; Tourismus-Information Hohenfurch, Tourist-Information Schongau: S. 81, 82, 83, 84; Verkehrsamt Peiting, Tourist-Informationsbüro Rottenbuch: S. 86; Verkehrsverein Wildsteig, Touristinformation Steingaden S. 91; Gästeinformation Halblech: S. 92; Tourist-Information Schwangau S. 95, 102; Kinkelin, Worins S. 95; Wittelsbacher Ausgleichsfonds München S. 99, 100, 101; Tegelbergbahn S. 102; Füssen Tourismus&Marketing: S. 108; Festspielhaus Neuschwanstein: Umschlagseite; Bayerische Zugspitzbahn Bergbahn AG: S. 110, 111.
Alle anderen Aufnahmen im Archiv des Herausgebers.

ISBN 978-3-940391-99-5